Essential Land Law for SQE1

Essential Land Law for SQE1 explains the key principles of Land law in a clear, easy-to-follow style. Principles are introduced and illustrated with reference to practical examples. The book demonstrates the skills of understanding and analysing the law, taking a clear and structured approach to analysing the facts, and then applying the relevant principles. It also includes a range of supportive features:

- Revision points: Each chapter concludes with a concise list of key revision points.
- Problem questions: To test understanding and analytical skills applied to practical scenarios. The SQE1 companion website provides suggested answers.
- Multiple choice questions: Each chapter of the book provides multiple choice questions following the SQE1 question format (with answers in an appendix to enable you to test your knowledge).

Part of Routledge's Essential Law for SQE1 series, this concise and accessible text provides a clear understanding of the Land law element of SQE1 and enables you to test your assessment skills. Without the assumption of any prior knowledge of Land law, it is suitable for both undergraduates and non-law graduates.

Mohammad Sabuj is a barrister (Lincoln's Inn) and Lecturer in Law at Royal Holloway, University of London, UK.

Essential Law for SQE1

Series editor: Wendy Laws

Essential Law for SQE1 is a series of concise textbooks aligned to the latest SQE1 curriculum. Providing candidates with an accessible summary of the core principles in each area of law, the style of each book is precise, with bullet-point lists summarizing key information and revision points concluding each chapter. The books also feature multiple choice questions with answers, example problem questions and a glossary of key cases.

For more information about this series, please visit: https://www.routledge.com/Essential-Law-for-SQE1/book-series/SQE1

Essential Tort Law for SQE1
Wendy Laws

Essential Dispute Resolution for SQE1
Ben Waters

Essential Business Law and Practice for SQE1
Bill Davies

Essential Land Law for SQE1
Mohammad Sabuj

Essential Land Law for SQE1

Mohammad Sabuj

Routledge
Taylor & Francis Group
LONDON AND NEW YORK

Designed cover image: Dimiraira / Getty Images

First published 2023
by Routledge
4 Park Square, Milton Park, Abingdon, Oxon OX14 4RN

and by Routledge
605 Third Avenue, New York, NY 10158

Routledge is an imprint of the Taylor & Francis Group, an informa business

British Library Cataloguing-in-Publication Data
A catalogue record for this book is available from the British Library

ISBN: 978-1-032-07005-6 (hbk)
ISBN: 978-1-032-07003-2 (pbk)
ISBN: 978-1-003-20495-4 (ebk)

DOI: 10.4324/9781003204954

Typeset in The Sans
by Deanta Global Publishing Services, Chennai, India

Access the SQE Companion Website here: https://routledgetextbooks.com/textbooks/sqe/

Contents

Table of cases

Table of statutes

Glossary

A

Absolute title A title to land which has satisfied all the legal requirements to become an absolute title. An absolute title is free from any qualifying condition or onward chain.

Actual occupation A person is in actual occupation where s/he holds a proprietary interest in a piece of land which is protected by actually occupying the land as opposed to merely receiving rents and profits of the land per se. An actual occupation as a valid **overriding interest** requires not only that the person is actually in occupation of the land but also that the interest is discoverable (an objective test) and within the actual knowledge of the transferee who paid valuable consideration.

Adverse possession Adverse possession is a right of a person to the property of another which can arise by adversely possessing the other person's property for a qualifying period of time, i.e., 10 or 12 years. The adverse possession must be without the consent and against the will of the real/paper owner. In other words, the requirements for possession are namely, 'without force, without secrecy, and without permission'. After completing the qualifying period an adverse possessor can become an owner of the property subject to completing the legal procedural requirement such as **registration**. Adverse possession is also known as squatter's right.

Advowson The right given to a bishop to live in the church premises.

Agreed notice This is a right or interest in a property that can be registered in the land **register** as a **notice** with agreement between **the registered proprietor** of the land and the holder of the right or interest. For instance, a notice is agreed where the **registered proprietor** of a land has agreed with the person who is in **actual occupation** of the property that the latter can enter the notice in the land **register**, or the **registrar** is satisfied with the validity of the applicant's claim.

Annexation Annexation is an inclusion or attachment of a right or thing to the land. The degree of annexation can be the decisive factor whether something attached to the land is a **fixture** or **chattel**. For instance, a bookshelf attached to the wall with screws can be a **fixture** or **chattel** depending on the degree of annexation. Annexation is also relevant in **freehold covenant** where the land benefitting from the covenant must show annexation of the benefit with the land.

B

Bare licence A bare **licence** is a permission given by the **licensor** without asking for any money or favour in return. For instance, a neighbour giving permission to another neighbour to park the latter's car in the former's parking space for a couple of days.

Beneficial interest Beneficial interest can exist in a land where the legal interest is vested in a **trustee** under a **trust**, but the beneficial interest is vested in the **beneficiaries**. The beneficial interest can be held by a person whose name does not appear in the title deeds or the land register as the owner or proprietor. However, their interest is held on **trust** by those whose name appears in the title documents. An example of a beneficial interest can be a spouse who has contributed to the purchase price of a property, but his/her name has not been included in the title documents. So, they hold a beneficial interest in the property.

Beneficiary The holder of a beneficial interest is known as a beneficiary. See also beneficial interest.

Benefitted land A benefitted land is that piece of land which receives benefits from a **freehold covenant** or **easement**.

Bona fide In good faith.

Break clause A break clause can exist in a contract outlining a situation or condition which can trigger termination of the contract. A **lease**, for instance, is terminable by a break clause before the end of the maximum duration. A grant of a **lease** for ten years can include a break clause which gives either party an option to terminate the **lease** by giving six months' notice once the period of seven years is completed under the **lease**.

Burdened land A burdened land is that piece of land which discharges a burden under a **freehold covenant** or **easement**.

C

Charge A charge is a burden registered over a property. For instance, a charge can be a debt taken against a property which is given as a security for the debt.

Charges register A register where **charges** can be registered. There are different registers for registering charges in **registered** and **unregistered** land.

Charitable corporation A charitable corporation is a charitable organisation registered as a charity in England and Wales with limited liability. For instance, the National Trust.

Chattel A chattel is something attached or annexed to the land but for the convenient use of the owner/occupier. For instance, a ceiling fan fitted in the bedroom.

Common intention Intention by or on behalf of both parties.

Common law Common law has been developed by judges in the English legal system for centuries based on customary and judicial decisions. This is separate from statutory law but in the modern world many common law principles have been adopted in the **statutes**.

Consideration Consideration is a key element in the formation of a contract. In a contract, one of the parties offers consideration for the other party to make a promise. So, a consideration must be something of a value. For instance, in a contract to buy a piece of land the buyer agrees to pay the purchase price as a consideration in exchange of a promise made by the seller who agrees to sell the land.

Constructive trust Where two or more people have directly or indirectly contributed to the purchase price of a property and had a **common intention** or agreement between them about the size of their respective shares in the property, a constructive trust occurs. Whereas direct payment to the purchase price includes payment towards the deposit, indirect payment includes mortgages, bills, repairs, and other household expenditures such as childcare expenses.

Conveyancing Also *Conveyancer* The activity of buying, selling, and transferring properties. The person who carries out this activity is known as a *conveyancer.*

Co-ownership Where two or more people own one or more property together.

Covenantee A person who is the owner of the **benefited land** and to whom a promise is being made. An original **covenantee** is a person who agreed to entertain the benefits for the first time under a covenant.

Covenantor A person who is the owner of a **burdened land** and who made the promises under a **covenant**. An original **covenantor** is a person who agreed to discharge a burden for the first time under a **covenant**.

Covenants **Covenants** are restrictions imposed on the property such as you cannot run a business. A **covenant** can be positive also such as 'to maintain the garden'.

Customary rights Rights of historic origin exercisable by inhabitants of a particular local area, such as the right to play sports on a piece of land or the right to hold an annual fair.

D

Declaration of trust A declaration of **trust** can be made when (i) the creator of a **trust** declares it formally in writing; or (ii) when a court declares a **trust** as valid.

Damages Damages are monetary compensation paid for a mistake made or wrong committed.

Declaration of title When a title is confirmed by the land **register** or a tribunal or a court.

Deed Written document that transfers a title in land. This must be signed and witnessed by a person of sound mind and full age.

Detriment Detriment is a loss suffered by a person.

Discretion A power of a judge or land **registrar** to decide a case or dispute or application by applying non-binding principles such as social or economic benefit, personal hardship, etc.

Dispositions Dispositions are transfers of land such as sale, mortgage.

Diversity of occupation Two or more people occupy a property or piece of land. For instance, the southern plot by a **tenant** and the northern plot by a **freeholder**.

Doctrine of notice Doctrine of notice applies to **unregistered** land under which a purchaser of a land can escape liability of a **third-party** interest if s/he purchases a **legal estate** in land in a good faith without notice of the third party's interest. The purchaser is also known as '**Equity**'s darling'.

Dominant land/tenement Dominant land is a piece of land that benefits from a right of **easement** such as a right of way over the neighbour's land.

E

Easements A **proprietary** right which enables a proprietor of an **estate** to make some limited use of land belonging to someone else. Examples include a right of way, right to light.

Electronic conveyancing Land **Registry** used the term 'electronic conveyancing' to describe a process of dealing with land whereby all or part of the **disposition** occurs online.

Equity's darling See 'Doctrine of notice'.

Estate A right to a piece of land that confers use or possession of the land for a period of time. For instance, the **freehold estate** (which has a potentially indefinite duration) and the **leasehold estate** (which lasts for a fixed duration). Those who hold a **freehold** or long **leasehold estate** are colloquially known as owners of land.

Estate contract A contract for the creation or transfer of an **interest** or **estate** in land, for example, a contract for sale or an agreement for a **lease**. The term also includes options to purchase and rights of pre-emption. An **estate** contract is an **equitable** interest in land.

Estoppel Estoppel is an informally created right by a promisor who promised a person to confer certain rights in a property. If the promisee (the person to whom the promise is made) suffered detriment from the reliance of the promise, then an estoppel would stop the promisor from reverting back from the promise.

Equitable Rights and interests in land that were historically recognised by particular courts, known as the Courts of **Equity**, and are now recognised by courts in the exercise of their **equitable** jurisdiction. Like legal interests, **equitable** interests confer a right over land that the person with the benefit of the interest does not own. Under section 4(1) of the Law of Property Act 1925, new types of equitable interests may only be created by statute.

Equitable easements These are **easements** which have not been created by a **deed** and registered in the Land **Registry**. Please note that an **equitable easement** can be entered in the **register** as a **notice** which is not similar to **registration** but just an entry.

Equity **Equity** recognises rights and interests which did not comply with the legal formalities. Such as a **beneficial interest** under a **trust** is recognised by **equity**. See beneficial interest.

Evidential burden This is a burden to provide evidence in support of an argument or claim.

Exclusive occupation Exclusive occupation is the right to occupy a property or part of a property without unreasonable or excessive interference from the landlord or anyone else. For instance, if you occupy a hotel room which is allocated to you as an employee of the hotel, this is an exclusive occupation of the room. You may be asked to leave the occupation once your employment is ended, or your employment contract is changed.

Exclusive possession Exclusive possession is a key criterion for a tenancy. In an exclusive possession a tenant can exclude anyone including the landlord from coming into the land without permission and such permission can be withheld or denied unless the tenant received a reasonable notice requesting access to the property.

F

Fee simple An **estate** in land potentially lasts forever. A fee simple is one of the two legal estates in land which can be registered with its own title (the other being certain leasehold estates).

First registration The registration of an **unregistered** land in the land register for the first time.

Foreclosure A right of a borrower to redeem the **mortgage** even after defaulting in making repayments.

Freehold *also* **Freeholder** An **estate** in land which potentially lasts forever. A freeholder is the highest interest holder in a land. They can create leasehold interest out of a freehold land. See also *fee simple*.

Fixture A fixture is something attached or annexed to a piece of land for the convenient use of the land. For instance, a fitted kitchen or window.

Forfeiture An action taken by a landlord to terminate a **lease** where the tenant or **lessee** fails to comply with a fundamental condition of the **lease**, i.e., keep up the payment of rent. A tenant can also invoke this method of termination of a **lease** where the landlord fails to keep up the repairs agreed under a **lease** agreement.

G

General equitable charge This is an **equitable** charge registered or registerable against a property, and/or **overreachable**. For instance, a **beneficiary's** right can be registered as a general **equitable charge** against the property which is held under a **trust**, and/or this **beneficial interest** can be **overreached**. See also, *overreaching, beneficial interest.*

Good leasehold title A good leasehold title arises when the title complies with the legal requirements for creating a valid lease. For instance, when a person with a more extensive estate in the land (the landlord or **lessor**) grants a right to exclusive possession of the land for a term to another person (the tenant or **lessee**).

Good root of title The records of title holders or owners of an **unregistered** land that date back to 15 years.

Grant The express or implied creation of an **estate** or interest in land, for example, a **lease** or an **easement**.

H

Hereditaments *also* **Corporeal/incorporeal** These are **estates** and interests in a property that can be inherited by a successor. Hereditaments can be corporeal, i.e., a land or building, and incorporeal, i.e., a rent.

Head-leaseholder A head-leaseholder is a person who has assigned a **lease** which is shorter than his/her **lease** period. For instance, a head-leaseholder of a **leas**e of 125 years can assign a 120-year **lease** to a **lessee**.

Home right A statutory right of occupation under Section 30 of the Family Law Act 1996. The right enables a spouse or civil partner to occupy a family home which is the matrimonial home or civil partnership home (as the case may be).

I

Implied trust A **trust** created impliedly. For instance, where a married couple bought a property together but only one of them was included in the title deeds or land **register** as owner. In this situation, an implied **trust** is created by conduct of the parties where the spouse whose name is included in the title **deeds** or land **register** held the other spouse's beneficial interest under an implied **trust**.

Imputed notice A notice is imputed where a person would have discovered a property right or interest if s/he had conducted a reasonable inquiry about the property. Therefore, a failure to conduct a reasonable inquiry by a person can impute a notice on him/her of an existing right or interest in the property which could have been discovered by such inquiry. An imputed notice can apply to the '**doctrine of notice**'.

Inheritance Succession

J

Joint tenancy A joint tenancy exists where the **co-owners** of a property have not identified their size of shares in the property. A joint tenancy can exist in **law** and **equity**. The right of **survivorship** applies to a joint tenancy which means that if one of the joint tenants dies his/her share goes to the surviving joint tenants.

L

Land charges Land charges are **third-party** rights or interests in a land which can be registered in the land **charges register**. Please note that the registers of land **charges** for **registered** and **unregistered** land are completely different. Examples of land charges are **estate** contracts, home rights, general **equitable** rights.

Land registry The office where rights and interests in a land are registered.

Lease An **estate** in land of a fixed duration, arising when a person with a more extensive **estate** in the land (the landlord or **lessor**) grants a right to **exclusive possession** of the land for a term to another person (the tenant or **lessee**). Legal **leases** are one of two **estates** in land which can be registered with their own title (the other being the **freehold estate**).

Lease for life Section 149(6) LPA 1925 which provides that a 'lease for life' granted at a rent or for a premium is converted to a lease for 90 years terminable by death (if earlier).

Leasehold See *lease*.

Licence A permission to do something on another's land which would otherwise amount to a **trespass**. A licence confers no **proprietary** right in the land.

Licensor A licensor is a person who grants the **licence**. See also *licence*.

Licensee A licensee is a person who receives a benefit under a **licence**. See also *licence*.

Life tenant A life tenant is a person who has a **tenancy** that can run as long as they are alive. The life **tenancy** ends with their death.

Legal right/interest One of the limited number of rights affecting land (listed in section 1(2) of the Law of Property Act 1925) which are recognised by the **common law** jurisdiction of the courts. Interests confer a right over land that a person with the benefit of the interest does not own. For example, a right of way.

Legal easements These are easements which have been created by a **deed** and registered in the Land **Registry**. Please note that a **legal easement** can be impliedly created such as by long use and in that case, it is automatically legal and there is no need to register.

Limited owner's charge This is a **charge** of a **life tenant** who has paid an inheritance tax under the Inheritance Tax Act 1984. In **unregistered** land, this charge can be registered as a class C (ii) land **charge** under section 2 (4) of the LCA 1972.

Lessor Owner of a leasehold property. Also known as a landlord.

Lessee **Tenant** of a leasehold property. Also known as a *tenant*.

M

Mortgage A debt or loan on the property against which money has been borrowed from a lender to pay the purchase price of the property.

Mortgagor A person who borrows money under a *mortgage*.

Mortgagee A person or organisation that lends money under a **mortgage**.

N

Notice Entry of third-party rights in the **land register**, i.e., **actual occupation**.

Nuisance Causing an undue interference in the enjoyment of a piece of land. For instance, by excessive noise.

O

Overriding interest An interest which is binding on a **registered proprietor** following the **first registration** of an **estate** in land, or a subsequently registered transfer of an already registered **estate** or **charge**, notwithstanding that the interest has not been noted in the **register**. For instance, rights of a person in **actual occupation**, short **leases** for seven years or less to run, impliedly created **easements**.

Option to purchase An option to purchase is a right of a **tenant** to buy a **freehold** or head-leasehold of a land at the end of the **tenancy**.

Overreaching The doctrine of overreaching is a means by which some **interests** in land, particularly **beneficial interests** under a **trust**, are removed from the land on a disposition and attached to the proceeds of sale.

P

Personal property *also* **Personalty** A personal property or personalty is a moveable asset or thing which exists as an action but not a realty. For instance, a credit balance in your account is a personalty which exists as a moveable asset.

Possessory title One of the classes of title with which a proprietor may be registered (see also **absolute title** and **qualified title**). Registration with possessory title does not affect the enforcement of any **estate**, right, or **interest** adverse to, or in derogation of, the proprietor's title subsisting at the time of registration.

Prescription Acquisition of rights by long use. For example, a right of way which has been acquired by virtue of usage of the way for the requisite period.

Periodic tenancy A **tenancy** that renews after a specific period for instance each month.

Practical benefit It is a benefit for which a restrictive covenant can be modified or discharged by the court. For instance, if removing the restriction 'not to run a business in the property' would bring a practical benefit to the area or locality then the court may exercise its discretion to modify or discharge the covenant.

Prima facie The first impression or primary position of a dispute.

Profits See ***profits à prendre***.

Profits à prendre A proprietary right to remove the products of natural growth from someone else's land; a common example is a right to cut turf, or to take game or fish. Unlike an easement, a profit need not benefit an estate in land.

Proprietary A right that binds the whole world, not only the parties who created it. For instance, a lease binds the whole world including a new purchaser of the leasehold land who was not a party to the lease.

Proprietary estoppel A proprietary estoppel creates an implied equitable right in a property where the owner promised someone that the latter would have a right in the property if they did do or did not do certain things, and they acted on the promise. For instance, the owner of a farm promised to his niece that the latter would have a right in the farm if she left her current job and moved into the farmhouse to look after the farm. In this situation, the niece can make a claim under 'proprietary estoppel' if the farm owner did not keep his promise. Under the 'estoppel' the farmer will be stopped from refusing to keep up the promise made to the niece who relied on that and acted accordingly to her detriment.

Privity of contract The legal relationship between the parties in a contract. The parties are bound by the terms of the contract because they have agreed to those. Therefore, each party is a privy to the contract. A privity of contract does not exist beyond the original parties.

Public benefit Public benefit can be a ground based on which a court can modify or discharge a restrictive covenant. For instance, a 'restriction not to build houses in an area' can be discharged or modified by the court if allowing to build in that area can bring a public benefit such as tackling homelessness.

Public right A right which members of the public have over land. For instance, a pedestrian's public right to access a path that runs across a park.

Puisne mortgage A second legal mortgage (charge) where the lender is not holding the title deeds to the land against which the charge is made.

Q

Qualified title One of the classes of title which a proprietor may be registered with (see also **absolute title** and **possessory title**). Registration with qualified title does not affect the enforcement of any **estate**, **right**, or **interest** which appears from the register to be excepted from the effect of **registration**.

Quasi-easement An **easement** right recognised by **common law** which can be impliedly created by a common owner of a land when s/he sold part of that land to another person. Once that part is sold, the new owner can claim quasi-easement of those easement-like rights that the common owner enjoyed before selling the part of the land if those rights were continuous, apparent, and necessary for the reasonable enjoyment of the part sold.

R

Real property *also* **Realty** Immoveable property such as a land, a building, or part of a building.

Rectification Amendment of the land **register** to correct a mistake.

Repudiatory breach of contract A breach that can trigger a claim for a breach of contract. For instance, where a landlord continuously failed or refused to carry out repairs of the property under the terms of a **lease** or statutory provision.

Register The land **register** where rights and interests in a land can be registered.

Registered proprietor The person whose name is registered in the land **register** as a proprietor.

Registrar The person in charge with the entry, update, and amendment of the land **register**.

Registration of land *also* **Registered land** The act of registration of rights and/or interests created, transferred, or modified in respect to a **registered** land.

Right of entry This is a right to enter the property. This right may be available to a landlord in order to repair the property. This right may also be available to a person who can enter a property to collect produces or deliver things (see also *profits á prendre*). For instance, a right of entry by a postman into your front garden to deliver the post.

Reservation An **easement** can be impliedly created by a reservation where the owner of a large piece of land sold part of that land and reserved an **easement** right, i.e., a right of way, over the part sold for the reasonable enjoyment of the retained land.

Restriction An entry in the **register** that regulates the circumstances in which a **disposition** of a registered **estate** or **charge** can be the subject of an entry in the **register**. For instance, a restriction based on a **beneficial interest** under a **trust** for **overreaching** purposes.

Restrictive covenant A **covenant** that restricts or prohibits certain activities in a piece of land, for instance, you cannot run a business. This is also known as a 'negative **covenant**'.

Resulting trust Where two or more people bought a piece of land but did not decide their respective size of shares at the time of purchase, the law assumes a **resulting trust** where their shares will be allocated according to the size of their contribution to the purchase price of the property.

Reversionary lease A **lease** that takes effect on a future date after its creation. This is usually a **lease** where the **lessee** agrees to go into possession of the property after more than three months from the date of the creation.

Rent control The control of rent by **statutes** such as the Rent Acts.

S

Servient land/tenement A land that bears the burden of discharging an **easement**.

Settlor The creator of a trust. See also *trusts*.

Severance The process by which a **joint tenancy** can become a **tenancy in common**.

Specific performance Performance of a contract exactly according to the promises made.

Survivorship The right of survivorship applies to a **joint tenancy** which means that if one of the joint tenants dies his/her share goes to the surviving **joint tenants**. See also *joint tenancy*.

Statute Act of parliament.

Statutory protection Protection available under a **statute**.

T

Tenancy in common Where a land is held under **tenancy in common**, each owner has an identifiable '*undivided share*' which s/he can sell, transfer, leave by will, etc. This means that the owners know the size of their shares but do not know which part of the property they own. For instance, the **co-owners** know that they each own 50% of the property but they do not know whether that 50% is from the east or west side of the land. Unlike **joint tenancy**, the right of **survivorship** does not apply to **tenancy in common**.

Tenancy See *lease*.

Tenant A holder of a **tenancy**.

Tenure A regime in which a person holds a land. For instance, a **freehold** tenure means that the holder of the tenure can hold the land almost forever.

Term of years See *leasehold*.

Third-party rights and interests Rights and interests in a property which can exist beyond the seller and buyer of a property. For instance, a personal in **actual occupation**, a **beneficial interest** under a **trust**, a right under **proprietary estoppel**.

Time orders Court orders that allow time for the repayments of **mortgages** by defaulted **mortgagors**.
Title deeds Property papers showing who holds the title.
Trespass Entering someone else's land without permission or a right to entry.
Trusts A legal relationship by which land is held in law by up to four persons (known as **trustees**) for the benefit of themselves or others (those with the benefit are called **beneficiaries**). The **trustees** have powers of management and sale, while the **beneficiaries** have the right to enjoy the land, either through occupation or receipt of profits and the proceeds of sale.
Trustee The holder of legal interest in a trust property. See also *trusts*.
Trustee in bankruptcy An administrator who takes charge of a bankrupt's assets.

U

Unregistered land Land with a title that is not registered in the **Land Registry**.
Unilateral notice This is a right or **interest** in a property that can be entered in the land **register** as a **notice** without agreement between the registered proprietor of the land and the holder of the right or **interest**. For instance, a **notice** is unilateral where the **registered proprietor** of a land has not agreed with the person who is in **actual occupation** of the property to enter the **notice** in the land register. As a result, the person in **actual occupation** has applied for a **unilateral notice** to enter in the land **register**. Contrast see *agreed notice*.
Unconscionability *also* **Unconscionable** Unfairness on a party to a dispute. For instance, if a borrower borrowed money by fraudulently representing that the borrowing was a personal loan where the money borrowed was in fact paid to buy a property the court can exercise its **discretion** to give effect a **mortgage** as otherwise it would be **unconscionable** for the lender.

V

Vice versa The other way around.
Vendor Seller.

W

Will A gift of a property by the owner which must be made in writing and witnessed by two people of full age and sound mind. A will takes effect after the death of the maker.

Introduction

This book provides a clear, concise explanation of key principles of Land law. Its focus is on those areas which fall within the assessment specification for the **Solicitors Qualifying Examination Part 1 Functioning Legal Knowledge** ('SQE1').[1]

In so doing, it also covers the areas of Land law central to most undergraduate Land law modules (and, for this purpose, it also includes coverage of proprietary estoppel, and adverse possession).

The style of the book reflects the SQE1 assessment specification:

- The SQE1 assessment requires knowledge and understanding of fundamental legal principles and the ability to apply them.
- Candidates are not required to recall specific case names or statutory provisions (except where they are normally used in practice to describe a legal principle).
- Candidates will be tested on the current law and will not be tested on the historical development of the law.

In order to reflect these requirements, the book explains the current key principles of Land law in a clear, easy-to-follow style. Principles are introduced and illustrated by reference to realistic factual examples. References to key cases and statutes are provided, but discussion of case law is reserved to the final section of the book (in an appendix).

This approach enables the book to provide a fluent narrative account of key principles which is clear and accessible, making it easier for the reader to understand the principles, remember them, and apply them in an assessment. For this purpose, a **glossary** section is dedicated to defining the key terminologies commonly used in Land law. These terminologies are also highlighted (**in bold**) in the text throughout the book.

1 See: SQE1 Functioning Legal Knowledge Assessment Specification, updated 14 October 2020, published by the Solicitors Regulation Authority, available via www.sqe.sra.org.uk/exam-arrangements/assessment-information/sqe1-assessment-specification.

The final section of the book then introduces key case law, following a structured format which enables the reader to examine the application of key principles of Land law in the context of decided cases.

Solicitors Qualifying Examination – SQE1

This book covers the areas of Land law in the **SQE1** assessment specification:

- Registered and unregistered land.
- Freehold and leasehold estates.
- Legal and equitable interests in land.
- Landlord and tenant (The Law of Leases).
- Co-ownership.
- Easements.
- Freehold covenants.
- Mortgages.

It also covers **licences and proprietary estoppel**, since these are recognised as essential backgrounds for understanding the areas of Land law covered by the SQE1 assessment specification. In addition, the book covers **adverse possession**. The assessment specification for SQE1 does not include these topics. However, they are included in this book because they often form part of undergraduate Land law modules.

Key features to assist learning

Revision points: Each chapter concludes with a concise list of key revision points.

Multiple choice questions: The SQE1 assessment uses multiple choice questions to test understanding of key principles. Multiple choice questions, following the SQE format, are provided at the end of each chapter of the book (with answers at the end of the book).

A further set of review multiple choice questions and answers is provided at www.routledge.com/cw/sqe.

Summary of cases: This book is different from existing textbooks or revision guides in that, instead of presenting a case-by-case account of the historical development of Land law, it provides a fluent narrative account of key principles, without discussing the underlying case law from which such principles are drawn. This approach was chosen specifically to fit the requirements of the SQE examination in which students are not expected to cite case law authorities. The benefit of this approach is that it enables the book to give a fluent explanation of principles which is clear, concise, and accessible. However, this book provides a case name or statutory provision where it is normally used in practice to describe a legal principle such as *Stack v Dowden*. This makes it easier for the reader to understand the principles, remember them, and apply them in the assessment. Also, a concise summary of cases is included in an appendix at the end of this book where the readers can find the facts of key decided cases, issues, judgment, reasoning, and additional comments (where appropriate).

Problem questions: Problem questions are provided to enable readers to test their knowledge and understanding of the Functioning Legal Knowledge (FLK) in which SQE1 candidates are assessed. Answers are available at www.routledge.com/cw/sqe.

The law is stated as at 22 December 2022.

1 Preliminary information before you start studying Land law for SQE1

Chapter overview

This chapter has been designed to provide you with some preliminary but very important information that you MUST know and understand before you start studying Land law for SQE1. You should have many questions about the requirement of the SQE1 for Land law, and how to prepare for assessment. This chapter aims to answer the questions that you may have in relation to Land law assessments for SQE1. This chapter also offers you to read and understand some key concepts of Land law and a very brief account of its evolution which you should find very useful throughout your journey of gaining a functional legal knowledge of Land law. In this chapter, you will also find a list of the relevant chapters that you must study to prepare for SQE1 assessment.

1.1 A suggested approach to studying Land law for SQE1

The nature of SQE1 assessment for Land law has been confirmed by the Solicitors Regulation Authority (SRA). The subject areas for Land law are registered and unregistered land; freehold and leasehold estates, and legal and equitable interests in land; landlord and tenant; and co-ownership. You must demonstrate depth and breadth of knowledge in these areas of law that are in force in England and Wales. This is described as 'Functional Legal Knowledge (FLK) by the SRA. In addition, you must also demonstrate good knowledge and understanding of these areas of Land law in three statements of solicitor competence (SoSC), namely A4, A5, and B3.[1] These competences are required to the level of a newly qualified solicitor. Therefore, it is very important that you gain the necessary knowledge by reading and understanding key principles of Land law outlined in this book. Once you have the necessary knowledge and understanding of the law you shall be able to identify the core legal principles and rules that a candidate will be asked to apply to factual issues so as to produce a

1 A4, A5, and B3 statements include competencies in registered and unregistered land; freehold and leasehold estates, and legal and equitable interests in land; landlord and tenant; co-ownership.

DOI: 10.4324/9781003204954-1

solution which best addresses a client's needs and reflects the client's commercial and/or personal circumstances.

The key to being successful in Land law assessment for SQE1 is a solid knowledge and understanding of the relevant statutory and common law rules, coupled with an appreciation of how those rules fit together. Although you must study each topic separately, it is only at the end of studying the relevant chapters (see below for a list of the relevant chapters) that a full understanding of Land law is really possible, so it is very important for you to review and revise the topics on a regular basis, and after reading all the relevant chapters of this book it might be helpful to stand back from the subject and think about how the topics interrelate. Please note that many assessment questions will require the application of principles from more than one topic. For example, registration of title, can affect the answer to almost any question; and there are overlaps between the chapters on licences and co-ownership. Again, when you have finished all the relevant chapters, it would be useful to go back to the MCQs and problem questions in the earlier chapters and see whether you can now give a more detailed or different answer, in the light of subsequent chapters. You can do this by attempting or re-attempting the MCQs and problem questions that are made available for you in this book. The following are relevant chapters for you which you must read and understand chronologically:

- **Chapter 1: Preliminary information before you start studying Land law for SQE1**
- **Chapter 2: Unregistered Land law**
- **Chapter 3: Registration of title (registered land)**
- **Chapter 4: Co-ownership 1: Informal acquisition of title: Implied trusts**
- **Chapter 5: Co-ownership 2: Trusts of land**
- **Chapter 6: Landlord and tenant (the law of leases)**
- **Chapter 8: Easements and profits á prendre**
- **Chapter 9: Freehold covenants**
- **Chapter 11: Mortgages**

In the assessment, candidates are required to answer Multiple Choice Questions (MCQs) where each single best answer question is followed by five possible answers. Candidates should mark only one or more answers for each question. To help you practise SQE-style MCQs, each chapter of this book contains sample questions that you can answer. In this way you can test your knowledge and understating of the relevant areas of law. You may find it more helpful to work through the questions with your notes and books in front of you.

Additionally, you must also show competence in identifying and addressing ethical problems in realistic client-based situations. In order to assist you in understanding and competently dealing with ethical issues, this book offers discussion and signposts to ethical code of conduct for Solicitors.

This book helps you to develop a solid understanding of the foundations of English Land law and of the current legal principles and concepts in use today. It explores and examines the different forms in which property rights in land arise and the mechanism used to secure those rights. You will develop comprehensive knowledge and skills in the application of legal principles to solve problems in Land law and answer SQE-style Multiple Choice Questions. This book also provides you with a disciplined approach and logical analysis which would help you to develop the skill of thinking and answering questions correctly. However, it is important for you to note that Land law is full of categories and sub-categories: a successful answer to any question will depend upon accurate, comprehensive, and logical analysis of how the facts of the question fit into those categories. There are four key questions to ask in response to any Land law question, and you must always be prepared to answer them and to explain why the answers matter:

1. Is the title to the land **registered** or **unregistered**?
2. What interests may exist in the relevant land?
3. Is each of the possible interests **legal** or **equitable**?
4. Have any necessary steps been taken to protect each of the possible interests?

This book offers the functional legal knowledge in Land law that you would need to grasp to address the above questions competently so you can apply the relevant law in answering the assessment questions.

1.2 Land law reforms in the 20th and 21st centuries

The 20th century has seen key reforms in the modern Land law of England and Wales. These reforms include enactment of key statutes to regulate creation of rights and transfer of interests in land. The key legislation of the 20th century is the Law of Property Act 1925 (hereinafter referred to as LPA 1925). The LPA drastically reduced the number of **estates** and **third-party rights**[2] that may subsist at law and so reduced the number of interests that automatically bind a purchaser. According to Section 1 of the LPA 1925, 'the only legal estates capable of subsisting in law are:

1. **Fee simple** absolute in possession.
2. A **term of years** absolute.

The only interests capable of subsisting in law are:

1. An **easement**.
2. A **rentcharge** in possession.

2 The terminologies in bold are defined in the 'glossary' section that is located in the front matter of this book.

3. A **charge** by way of legal **mortgage**.
4. **Rights of entry**'.

This section was introduced to prevent the parties from producing or inventing novel property rights. As a result, the nature and extent of any rights and interests in property must be one or more of those listed in Section 1 of the LPA 1925.

Another important piece of legislation, the Land Registration Act 2002 (hereinafter referred to as LRA 2002) was enacted at the beginning of the 21st century. The aim of the LRA 2002 was to ensure quick, efficient, and inexpensive transfer of estates and interests in land while ensuring third-party interests are properly protected. The fundamental objective of the LRA 2002 was that

> the register should be a complete and accurate reflection of the state of the title of the land at any given time, so that it is possible to investigate title to land online, with the absolute minimum of additional enquiries and inspections.[3]

The LRA 2002 came into force on 13 October 2003. The main changes introduced by the 2002 Act are as follows:

1. Changes to the nature and scope of **overriding interests** in registered land.[4]
2. A system of **electronic conveyancing** which will be phased in until it is universal.
3. Substantial changes to the law of **adverse possession** for registered land.
4. The expansion of the situations in which **registration of land** is compulsory, with a corresponding encouragement of voluntary land registration.
5. The creation of the new office of the Adjudicator to Her Majesty's Land Registry to deal with disputes about registered land.

Among these changes a few categories have not been carried out yet. For example, the aim to register rights and interests simultaneously with their creation and transfer (electronic conveyancing) has not taken place. In addition, the land register is yet to be a complete and accurate reflection of the state of title as there are **overriding interests** which still bind a new **registered proprietor**.

1.3 Identifying different rights and interests in land (freehold and leasehold estates)

There may be multiple rights and interests in a piece of land. If someone says that 'I own Greenacre', it does not mean that that person's ownership is not subject to any

3 Law Comm. No. 271, paragraph 1.5.

4 The statutory provisions in relation to 'overriding interests' are discussed in Chapter 3.

other rights or interests in the land. The owner of Greenacre may be bound by interests of other parties which the former has either expressly created or is impliedly bound by the law. Please see Figure 1.1.[5]

Figure 1.1 shows that an owner of a **freehold** piece of land can create other interests in the same land and be bound by those interests. For instance, an owner can grant a **lease** (Y), take a mortgage by securing Greenacre (Z), create express or implied **trusts** (T), grant a right of entry to a third party (E), or **an option to purchase** (D), sever his/her property interest and become co-owners. Similarly, an owner may be bound by rights of other people by operation of law. For example, the owner of Greenacre may be bound by an **estoppel** which s/he unknowingly created, or the owner of the Redacre (who can be a neighbour of the Greenacre) may be bound by a restrictive **covenant** such as not to run a business in the property that was passed on to him/her by operation of law. Moreover, the beneficial and reasonable enjoyment of the Greenacre and Redacre are protected by law such as an easement, e.g., right of way over a neighbour's land.

Therefore, it cannot be said that a freeholder absolutely owns Greenacre or Redacre. The right of a **freeholder** may be subject to rights of others such as the mortgagee bank. This freeholder's right may also be subject to other third-party interests, such as a tenant whose right is protected against a new freeholder who purchased the property from the tenant's landlord. The new landlord's right is subject to the remaining term of the tenancy unless the tenant decides to terminate the tenancy and reaches an agreement with the new freeholder.

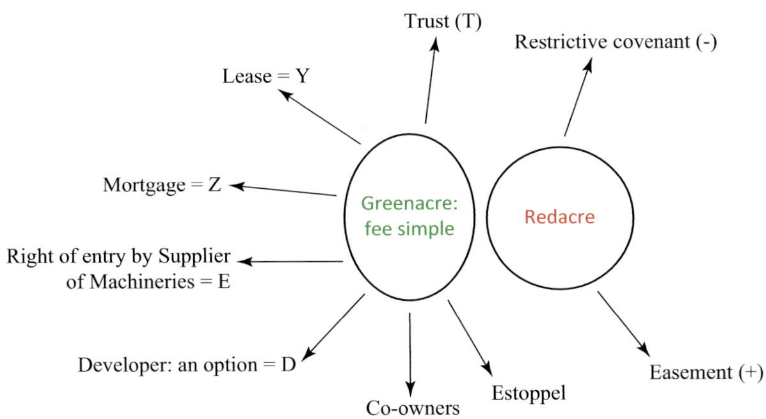

Figure 1.1 Different rights and interests in land.

5 There are diagrams and tables included in this book to outline the key principles of Land law.

1.4 Key concepts in Land law

1.4.1 What is land?

Section 205(1) (ix) LPA 1925 has defined 'land' as:

> land of any **tenure**, and mines and minerals, whether or not held apart from the surface, buildings or parts of buildings (whether the division is horizontal, vertical or made in any other way) and other **corporeal hereditaments**; also a manor, and **advowson**, and a rent and other **incorporeal hereditaments**.

When a buyer wants to buy a piece of land, they must know what is included in the land and what is not. The contract of sale does not contain an itemised list of what is and what is not included in the sale. As a result, a purchaser of land only gets what is included in the definition of land. The statutory definition of land only provides a list of the types of rights that are part and parcel of the land. However, this list is not exhaustive and ownership of anything attached to the land will depend on whether they are **fixtures** or **chattels**. Fixtures are included but chattels are not unless otherwise agreed between the buyer and the seller. Whereas fixtures are so eagerly attached to the land as they become part of the **real property**, chattels are also part of the land or attached to it but merely as a **personal property**. The following table shows the differences between real and personal property (see Table 1.1).

In Table 1.1, real property included those properties which are attached to the land. For instance, land, buildings, and fixtures i.e., window frames are attached to the land. On the contrary, most moveable properties which are commonly used for personal enjoyment of the land but NOT attached to the land are 'personal property', namely a freestanding wardrobe, a fridge, a washing machine, and the logo '7UP' in

Table 1.1 Differences between real property and personal property

Real property	Personal property
• Land. • Anything permanently attached to the land: ○ Buildings, structures, fixtures; ○ Water and water rights; ○ Minerals on and below the surface of the earth; ○ Trees and crops; ○ Airspace above the surface. • Both proprietary and personal rights exist.	• Anything other than real property: ○ Clothing, jewellery, furniture; ○ Electric and electronic appliances; ○ Equipment and machineries; ○ Copyrights, patents, and trademarks. • Must be delivered to change ownership. • Can be tangible or intangible. • No one except the owner has any right or interest.

a shop which is now being sold. The key difference between a 'real' and 'personal' property is that a sale of a piece of land only includes 'real property', NOT 'personal property', unless expressly included in the contract of sale.

The tests that apply to determine whether chattels have become fixtures are:

- the degree of **annexation**, and
- the purpose of annexation.
  - This test is used to ascertain whether the chattel has been fixed more for the convenient use of it as a chattel, or more for the convenient use of the land or building.
  - If the method of annexation is adopted for the enjoyment of the object as a chattel, then even a comparatively durable method of annexation will not render it a fixture.

Self-assessment question: Sanjay has entered a contract for the sale of his house to Peppa. He asks you whether the following items (which are not mentioned in the contract of sale) are to be included in the sale:

1. A statue standing in the garden.
2. A chandelier.
3. A fitted kitchen.
4. A radiator fitted into strips of metal screwed into the wall and connected to the central heating system.

1.4.2 Proprietary and personal rights

Proprietary rights are those rights which bind the whole world. For example, freehold and leasehold estates. On the contrary, **personal** rights are those which only bind the persons who entered into such a relationship. For example, a contractual **licence** between Charlotte and David, where the former agreed to occupy the latter's house in return of a weekly payment of £100. The legal position is that a proprietary right, such as a lease, is binding against the whole world, including any new owner who purchases the land subject to the lease. Conversely, a personal right, such as a contractual licence, is not binding against the new owner but between the parties themselves. The following table shows the characteristics of proprietary and personal rights in land (see Table 1.2).

In Table 1.2, the key difference between a proprietary and personal right is outlined. A right that binds the whole world and not only the parties who created it is a proprietary right. For instance, a lease binds the whole world, including a new purchaser of the leasehold land who was not a party to the lease. As a result of this, the leaseholder or tenant is protected from eviction by the new owner because the former's

Table 1.2 The characteristics of proprietary and personal rights in land

Proprietary	Personal
• Proprietary rights are enjoyed against the whole world. For example, if you own a property you are entitled to claim the title against the whole world. You lose the title as soon as you sell the property to someone else (lease). • Rights and interests recognised by the LPA 1925, e.g., estate in **fee simple**, leasehold interest, and rentcharges.	• Personal rights are only enforceable between the persons who agreed on an obligation in relation to land as opposed to against the whole world. These rights can also arise by operation of law. For example, a right of entry by a postman into your front garden to deliver the post (**licence**). • Rights/interests created out of contract only.

right is a proprietary right. On the contrary, a personal right can only bind the parties of a contract. For instance, if you buy a cinema ticket to watch a movie this is a contractual licence between you and the cinema and hence only a personal right. If the cinema management decides to cancel the showing of the movie your right to get a refund of the ticket price is only valid against the cinema, NOT the whole world.

1.4.3 Legal and equitable rights

As suggested in Section 1.1, you should always carefully look for the NATURE of the right (legal or equitable). This is because the status and enforceability of a right varies depending on whether it is a legal or equitable right. Whereas legal rights are protected by legislation or common law, equitable rights are more informal in nature and subject to the discretion of the judges.

The rights must be created in certain ways to be legal or otherwise they are equitable. For example, whether the formal procedural requirements have been fulfilled as required by statutes. If the formal procedure is not being followed the right cannot be legal but equitable. Therefore, a lease for more than seven years must be registered in order to be a legal lease.[6] If not registered, it will be an equitable lease. However, there are certain exceptions which you MUST know. For instance, a lease for three years or less is legal by default so it does not need to be made in writing or registered.[7]

6 Ss. 4(1) and 27(2)(b) of LRA 2002.

7 S. 1 of LP (MP) Act 1989 – written and executed by the right holder, and one witness (also known as by deed). **Exception**: short lease (three years or less) – Ss. 52(2) (d) and 54(2) of LPA 1925; and prescription (long use).

1.4.3.1 Tips on legal and equitable distinctions

- Always find out if the rights or interests are legal or equitable.
- If both are legal then both should be enforced.
- If both are equitable then the first in time shall prevail.
- If one is legal and another is equitable then the legal right shall prevail in LAND LAW.

Chapter revision points

- Rights and interests in land can be proprietary or personal.
- There can be legal and equitable rights in a property.
- Legal rights/interests: full formality is required.
- Equitable rights/interests: less formality is required.
  - No execution of deed.
  - No registration.
- Equitable rights must be created in an appropriate manner. If not, those rights will be mere personal rights such as a licence.

Multiple choice question

Sanjay is the registered proprietor of an old manor house with an oval shape garden around it. He wanted to attract potential caravaners to park their caravans in the garden of the house. He also wanted to rent out a few rooms of the house to holidaymakers. So, he decided to carry out some renovation works in the house and garden. The renovation works carried out included laying out of new carpets, fitting of a new central heating system, and installing pre-paid electric charging ports for the caravaners. Although the business was doing very well during the summer it suffered a loss during the winter and did not attract many holidaymakers and caravaners to the house and its adjoining garden. Hence, he decided to sell the house and garden. Peppa bought the house and garden but when moved in she found that Sanjay had removed the carpets, the radiators, the combi boiler from the central heating system, and the electric sockets from the property.

Which one of the following best explains the likely outcome for Peppa?

A. Sanjay needs to refit the carpets, reinstall the radiators, combi boiler, and electric sockets because these are fixtures and accordingly constitute parts of the land that were sold to Peppa.

B. Sanjay does not need to refit the carpets and reinstall the radiators, combi boiler, and electric sockets because these are chattels and accordingly do not constitute parts of the land that were sold to Peppa.

C. Sanjay does not need to refit the carpets or reinstall the electric sockets because these are chattels and accordingly do not constitute parts of the land that were sold to Peppa. However, he needs to reinstall the radiators and combi boiler as these are fixtures and accordingly constitute parts of the land.
D. Sanjay does not need to refit the carpets or reinstall the radiators and combi boiler because these are chattels and accordingly do not constitute parts of the land that were sold to Peppa. However, he needs to reinstall the electric sockets as these are fixtures and accordingly constitute a part of the land.
E. Sanjay does not need to reinstall the radiators, combi boiler, and electric sockets because these are chattels and accordingly do not constitute parts of the land that were sold to Peppa. However, he needs to refit the carpets as these are fixtures and accordingly constitute a part of the land.

Answer: See Appendix C.

2 Unregistered Land law

Chapter overview

This chapter deals with 'unregistered Land law'. It is very important for you to note that the laws relating to registered title land are very different from that of unregistered land. Whereas in the unregistered system a purchaser will require a vendor (seller) to show a **good root of title** for up to 15 years back, and hence a fresh investigation of title becomes necessary on each sale, in the registered system the legal title is investigated just once (by the Land Registrar) and then registered.

Although more than 87% of the land in England and Wales is registered,[1] the remaining land is not and the process of registering this unregistered land is very slow. Therefore, it is very important for you to understand the law relating to unregistered land that is still applicable in the current legal framework. Unregistered land is owned by institutions which need not sell or transfer their interest in land. For instance, land owned by a church or a university. Therefore, it is important for you to understand the application of the law in relation to unregistered land. Moreover, many principles of modern Land law emerged or evolved from the unregistered system of law which you would need to know in order to better understand the functioning of those principles.

This chapter discusses the issue of priority, doctrine of notice, and investigation of title in unregistered land. The issue of priority deals with questions such as when a new purchaser is going to be liable for any rights and interests in land which the seller was liable for. This question is very important as knowing the answer to this question will enable you to understand what checks are necessary before purchasing unregistered land. You would need to carry out certain checks, such as to see if anyone else other than the paper owner is living in the property. You need to know this because those people whose names are not included in the papers (**deed**) may have an interest which may be binding on you after buying the unregistered land. Checking whether anyone else other than the paper owner has any rights or interests in the land will make you understand the application of the '**doctrine of notice**'

1 HM Land Registry, available at www.gov.uk/government/organisations/land-registry/about (accessed 20 January 2022).

DOI: 10.4324/9781003204954-2

which is also known as 'equity's darling'. The answer to the question about the 'liability of a new purchaser of unregistered land' is heavily dependent on the 'doctrine of notice'. The chapter concludes with the necessary checks that a purchaser MUST carry out before purchasing unregistered land.

2.1 The issue of priority

Imagine that Jemina owns Greenacre (see Figure 2.1). She gives a right of way to her neighbour Noel across Greenacre, which he uses to get to the local shop. Jemina sold Greenacre to Umar.

Issue of priority:

- Can the existing right that Noel has in Greenacre be binding on Umar as the new owner?
- Can Noel continue to use the right of way or does he lose it when Umar buys the land?

According to the Law of Property Act 1925 (LPA 1925),[2] the issue of priority is subject to the following categories:

- Category 1: **Legal** rights with one exception.
- Category 2: **Equitable** rights in fact plus one legal right which are registrable as a **land charge** under the Land Charges Act 1972 (LCA 1972).
- Category 3: The right of the beneficiary under a trust who is not also the legal owner (also known as overreaching).
- Category 4: Equitable rights to which the doctrine of notice still applies (a residual category).[3]

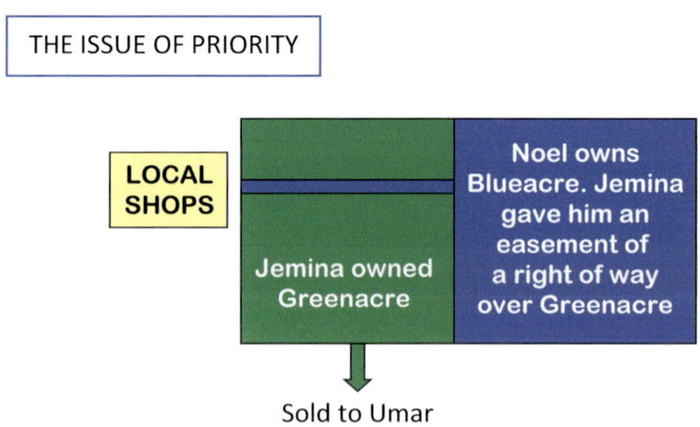

Figure 2.1 The issue of priority in unregistered Land law.

2 LPA 1925 came into force on 1 January 1926.
3 LPA 1925, S. 2(1).

In the first category, all legal rights have priority over any subsequently created legal rights. Therefore, legal rights are not required to be registered in order to have priority. It is important for you to note that only equitable rights need to be registered as land charges. Although land charges involve a certain type of registration, this has absolutely nothing to do with registered land itself. There is a quite separate register for unregistered land charges only. The register where these equitable rights can be registered is known as the 'charges register'. The entries in the register are known as land charges because a charge is a kind of burden on the land. In the above example, Noel can continue to exercise the right of way against Umar if this is a legal right (legal **easement**). This is based on the principle that 'legal rights bind the whole world'. The only exception is a 'first mortgage' which must be registered to be protected. A first **mortgage** is a **charge** on the property against which the money has been borrowed from the lender to pay the purchase price. The first mortgage must be registered because if it is not, then no purchaser would be able to know if the unregistered land is subject to a charge against which money has been borrowed from the lender. In order to protect a new buyer of unregistered land the first mortgage, although a legal right, must be registered to be protected.

In the second category, certain equitable rights listed in the LCA 1972 must be registered in order to have priority. For instance, according to S. 2 LCA 1972 the following rights must be registered in the **charges register**:

Class C(i) = **Puisne mortgage** [the one legal right].
Class C(iii) = **General equitable charge**.
Class C(iv) = Estate contract.[4]
Class D(ii) = **Restrictive covenant** made on/after 1/1/1926.
Class D(iii) = Equitable **easement** made on/after 1/1/1926.
Class F = **Home rights** – Matrimonial & Civil Partner's Home Rights (under Family Law Act 1996 as amended by the Civil Partnership Act 2004).[5]

Once the above equitable rights are registered, they are binding on any future purchasers of unregistered land. The register where these equitable rights can be registered is known as the 'charges register'. The entries in the register are known as land

4 Estate contract, for example, includes an option to purchase (a contract which provides that the seller is obligated to sell the land if the buyer chooses to buy it), and a first right to refuse to purchase (pre-emption). Pre-emption comes into play where the seller promises that if she decides to sell her legal estate within a certain number of years then she will offer it first to the buyer. So here the seller is in a stronger position. She doesn't have to sell unless she wants to, but if she decides that she is going to do so, then she must first offer the land to the buyer. For example, Jemina contracts to sell her legal estate in Greenacre to Umar. Under this contract she has to sell and Umar has to buy. This contract will have to be registered to have priority.

5 For an understanding of the application of the 'home rights', see <http://rightsofwomen.org.uk/get-information/family-law/marriage-your-rights-to-your-home/#What%20are%20home%20rights?> (accessed 10 October 2021).

charges because a charge is a kind of burden on the land. The register is open for inspection, so Noel can enter his equitable easement (right to cross the Greenacre) on the register to protect this, and similarly Umar can inspect the register to find out about this right. When Umar finds out about this right, he can then decide whether or not to go ahead with the purchase. However, we now need to consider the following questions:

Who must register it? As Jemina has given Noel the easement, it is Noel who would have to register this.

Who is this registered against? It is against the name of the estate owner whose estate is affected (in our example, Jemina). It is not against the address of the property. This is what Section 3(1) Land Charges Act 1972 says. In our example, Noel must register this right against Jemina's official name, which is 'Jemina Zakaria', NOT in the name she is commonly known to people like 'Jem Zakaria'.

Another relevant question is, what happens if a right is registered against a wrong name? This depends on whether or not the purchaser searched against the right name. If Umar searched the register against the right name which is 'Jemina Zakaria', then he is not bound where the right is registered against 'Jem Zakaria'. However, if Umar searched under a wrong name such as 'Jemie Zakaria', then he cannot rely on the search results. Therefore, you should search for a different version of a name, so in this case it is necessary to search 'Jemina Zakaria', 'Jem Zakaria', and also 'Jemie Zakaria' so the seller can be sure. However, searching for the official name of the seller (as seen in the birth certificate/passport) should suffice.[6]

Where a registerable right is registered as a land charge against the correct name then Section 198 Law of Property Act reveals the impact: *Registration should be deemed to constitute actual notice to all persons dealing with the land.*[7] So, if correctly registered, the equitable right will bind all future owners of the land. And the consequence for purchasers of the land is that they must check the Land Charges Register before buying the property, because they will be bound by any entry in the register, whether they made the search or not.

What happens if a right is not protected as a land charge when it should have been? Failure to register it will mean that it will not be binding against certain types of purchasers. Different rules apply for different classes of land charges as set out in Section 4 of the 1972 Land Charges Act. See Table 2.1.

6 *Diligent Finance Company v Alleyne* (1971) 23 P & CR 346; see also *Oak Cooperative Building Society v Blackburn* [1967] CH 730.
7 LPA 1925, S. 198.

Table 2.1 Categories of land charges and the effect of non-registration

Categories of land charges	Effect of non-registration
Class C(iv)	Void against a purchaser of a legal estate.
Class D(i), D(ii), D (iii)	
Class C(i), C(ii), C(iii)	Void against a purchaser of a legal or equitable estate.
Class F	

- Where the right should have been registered as a Class C(iv) – [estate contract], D(i) – [charge by HM Customs and Revenue], D(ii) – [Restrictive covenant made on/after 1/1/1926], or D(iii) – [Equitable easement made on/after 1/1/1926], it will be void against a purchaser of a legal estate for money. Void means not binding.[8] Thus an unregistered land charge within those classes will not be binding on a purchaser who satisfies 2 requirements – (a) they must buy a legal estate; and (b) they must pay money or money's worth. This means something which can be measured in financial terms, and if it can be measured financially, then it doesn't have to be adequate which means it can be worth less than what the land itself is worth in the market.[9]
- Where the right should have been registered as a Class C(i) – C(iii) – [**Puisne mortgage**, **limited owner's charge**, and general equitable charge] and a Class F – [home rights], it will not be binding on a purchaser of any estate or interest for valuable consideration.[10] This means that only a purchaser who has paid a purchase price for the property will be able to avoid liability but not a non-purchaser such as those who inherited the property or received it as a gift. In reality almost no purchaser would be bound if the interest was not registered.[11]

The knowledge by a purchaser of the existence of an unregistered land charge that should have been registered is irrelevant because Section 199(i) LPA 1925 states '*A purchaser shall not be prejudicially affected by notice of anything that is capable of registration as a land charge but which is void or not enforceable against him by reason of non-registration*'. So even actual knowledge is irrelevant. What matters is registration.[12]

8 LCA 1972, S. 4(6).

9 An estate contract or a restrictive covenant or an equitable easement will be void for non-registration against a purchaser of a legal estate for money or money's worth. So, a purchaser of an equitable lease or bank lending money by means of an equitable mortgage remains bound.

10 LCA 1972, S. 4(5) and 4(8).

11 A puisne mortgage or a general equitable charge or a spouse's right of occupation of the matrimonial home will be void for non-registration against any purchaser for value of the land or any interest in the land (whether legal or equitable estate or interest is purchased).

12 *Midland Bank v Green* [1981] AC 513.

The one legal right that has to be registered as a land charge is a '**puisne** (pronounced PUNY) **mortgage**. This is a second mortgage by the **mortgagor** (borrower) whereof the borrower deposited the property papers (**title deeds**) to the first **mortgagee** (lender) to secure the debt or loan taken to pay the purchase price of the property. Therefore, the second mortgage is nothing but another charge on the property.[13] The reason the first lender makes the borrower hand over their property papers is so that the borrower cannot sell the house behind the lender's back. The owner would need the papers before a purchaser could go ahead with the purchase. As a result, unlike the first lender, a second lender does not have that protection and so instead they are able to register their mortgage as a Class C(i) land charge (see Table 2.1). In summary, a **puisne mortgage** is a second legal mortgage where the lender is not holding the title deeds to the land against which the charge is made.

In the third category, a **beneficial interest** held under a **trust** is not registrable as a Class C (iii) – [general equitable charge] (see Table 2.1) land charge under the LCA 1972 but they are overreachable. **Overreaching**[14] can occur in a position where two people, Mike and Vicky for instance, both contributed to the purchase price of a property known as Pinkacre. But the property was put into Mike's name only. In this situation, we have a **trust** where Mike is the legal owner, holding the property on **trust** for himself and Vicky as beneficial owners. Now, what happens if Philip wants to buy the property? Well, the property has been put into Mike's name only. Therefore, he is the only one who needs to sign the paperwork known as 'Deed of Transfer'. It is important for you to know that the transfer deed is the document that transfers ownership from the seller to the buyer. Once Mike signs the transfer deed, all his interest transfers to the buyer. However, someone who is only a **beneficiary** and not also a **legal** owner does not need to sign the transfer deed, so their equitable right does not automatically transfer to the buyer. So, a beneficiary under a trust who is not also a legal owner, a person such as Vicky, can cause a problem for the buyer, because the latter could end up being bound by her beneficial right and this would mean that she could continue living in the property (see Figure 2.2). The solution from the buyer's perspective lies in this term *overreaching*. Overreaching allows the buyer to take free from the beneficiary's rights. In other words, once the beneficial interest is overreached this cannot bind a new purchaser.[15]

13 LCA 1972, S. 2 (4) (i).

14 The concept of 'overreaching' in unregistered land operates in the same manner as 'registered land'.

15 Overreaching applies only to family home NOT Commercial property. See also *Birmingham Midshires Mortgage Services Ltd* v *Sabherwal* [2000] 80 P&CR 256.

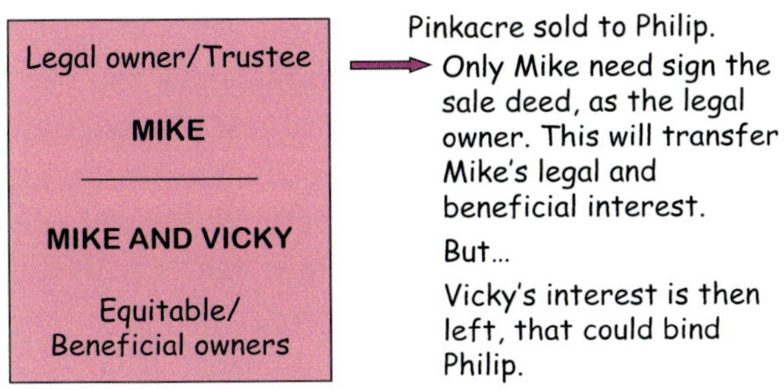

Figure 2.2 The situation where overreaching is concerned.

So, what action must be taken for overreaching to occur? Sections 2 and 27(2) LPA 1925 govern this. The purchaser must pay the purchase money to a minimum of two **trustees**, i.e., two people whose names are on the legal title. In return of the purchase money, the two trustees must give the purchaser a valid receipt for the purchase money that s/he has paid. On completion of this process, the purchaser will overreach the beneficiary's interest and the impact is that the beneficiary's interest is transferred off the land and into the sale proceeds. So, it is deflected off the land altogether and transferred into the proceeds of sale and the buyer is not bound. Also, you should consider the following questions:

What if there is just one trustee? Well, if that's so, then a second person must be appointed. So, in Mike and Vicky's case someone else, maybe a solicitor, would become the second trustee and their name would be put on the legal title alongside Mike.

Why must there be two trustees? Well simply it is thought that there is less risk of two people making off with purchase money and not compensating the beneficiary for their interest than if there is just one person. Also, when the purchaser buys the land then they need not have any concern about a person in Vicky's situation. Indeed, even if they know of the interest to the beneficiary, overreaching will still be effective. Finally, in the example between Mike and Vicky, the purchaser was an ordinary individual but note that overreaching can be used when a mortgage is created. Thus, for example, if Mike borrows money from a bank for home improvements, the bank would need to appoint a second trustee before it handed over the loan to avoid being bound by Vicky's interest.

The fourth category addresses the question what if the beneficial interest is not overreached by a purchaser? So, we now move on to the final category of rights that we need to be concerned with, *equitable interests to which the doctrine of notice still applies* (see Section 2.2). But before that, let's explore a few problems with the land charges system that applies to unregistered land only.

2.1.1 Problems with the land charges system

The land charges registration system has considerable advantages from the purchaser's point of view, in that it generally relieves him/her of the need to make inquiries and inspections of the land. Its major defect from the purchaser's point of view is that registration is not against the land (as is the case with registered land) but against the name of the estate owner. One estate may have been owned by many successive people since registration of land charges began, with the potential of land charges registered against each under his/her own name.

Since the LPA 1969 S. 23 reduced the length of title which has to be investigated in order to find a 'good root of title' to 15 years, it has become even more difficult for a purchaser to discover all the relevant names, yet s/he is still deemed to have actual notice of the charges registered against them (e.g. a **restrictive covenant** registered in 1930 against the name of the estate owner at that time). If bound by such a hidden interest then s/he may be entitled to compensation at public expense.[16] However, the number of claims for compensation is very small. For example, only one claim in the first 21 years has been made following the introduction of the scheme.[17]

2.2 Doctrine of notice – Equity's darling[18]

Since the enactment of the LPA 1925, the application of the 'doctrine of notice' has been very limited. The only residuary application of the 'doctrine of notice' is where the overreaching has failed under the third category (see example given in a box with sentence beginning 'In the third category'). Also, it applies to '**restrictive covenants** and **equitable easements**' created before 1 January 1926.

The doctrine of notice is also known as a '*bona-fide purchaser of the legal estate for value without notice of the equitable right*'. So, in the example given in Figure 2.2, if Vicky's interest is not overreached then a bona-fide purchaser of the legal state for value without notice of the equitable right cannot be bound by her interest. The elements of the doctrine can be broken down to the following parts:

- Bona fide.
- Purchaser for value.
- Of the legal estate.
- Without notice of the equitable right.

So, the requirements are that *firstly*, s/he is bona fide, meaning someone acting in good faith. *Secondly*, s/he must be a purchaser for value. So s/he must give either money or some other form of **consideration**. *Thirdly*, then s/he must be buying a

16 LPA 1969 S. 25.

17 Land Registry Annual Report 1989–1990, p 11.

18 For "Equity's darling" see the glossary; see also explanation at the end of this section.

legal estate, thus a legal **leasehold** or legal **freehold**. And *finally*, s/he must be without notice of the equitable right. Without notice means simply that the purchaser didn't know about the equitable right or interest. If they didn't know about it, they would not be bound. So, if Vicky can show that the purchaser knew about her equitable interest, then the latter will have to be bound by her beneficial interest. Note also that a purchaser for value includes a mortgagee. That is a person, a bank or building society who lent money and has a mortgage over the property. So, say for example Mike owns Greenacre and he borrows some money from the Mortgageway (a bank) for home improvements. He gives it a mortgage. If he does not repay the mortgage, the bank would take Greenacre away from him to try and sell it in order to recoup its money. The issue is, however, whether or not Mortgageway and whoever buys it from the bank is bound by Vicky's right or not.

Most new owners would in fact meet the requirements of being a bona fide purchaser of the legal estate. So, the test that really mattered was whether they have notice, which is why this rule is usually called the **doctrine of notice**. In fact, there are three types of notice namely; actual notice, constructive notice, and imputed notice.

- The first is 'actual notice' which means when the purchaser does have actual knowledge of the equitable right or interest.[19]
- The second is constructive notice. This is when the purchaser should have known of the equitable right or interest. We will look at this in a little more detail shortly.
- The third type is imputed notice. Where a purchaser has an agent such as a solicitor or a surveyor acting for them then the agent's actual or constructive notice of the equitable right or interest is treated as knowledge of the purchaser. That is, the agent's knowledge would be imputed to the purchaser.

S. 199 (1) (2) LPA 1925 explains when a constructive notice may arise. *A purchaser will have notice of any interest if it ... would have come to his knowledge if such enquiries and inspections had been made as ought reasonably to have been made by him.* The test is an objective one. Would all reasonable inquiries and inspections have revealed the right or interest? If yes, the purchaser is bound. If no, he is not bound. Even if he didn't actually make any inquiries, it doesn't matter if all reasonable inspections and inquiries wouldn't have shown the right up anyhow.

What type of inquiries and inspections need to be made to satisfy S. 199? These must at least include firstly to inspect the owner's title documents, i.e., the evidence that s/he owns the property because a purchaser is bound by any right s/he would have discovered if s/he had inspected the title deeds. Secondly, s/he must physically inspect the property.[20] The 'doctrine of notice' is known as the 'equity's darling'

19 S. 98 of LPA 1925 provides that 'registration shall be deemed to constitute actual notice' to all persons dealing with the land.
20 *Kingsnorth Finance Co. Ltd v Tizard* [1986] 1 WLR 783.

because it protects a buyer who buys a legal estate in good faith, for value, and does not have knowledge of the equitable right or interest in the property.

When there has been a bona fide purchaser for value of the legal estate without notice, no subsequent purchaser will be bound by the equitable right or interest that they avoided.[21] The presence of a bona fide purchaser destroys the equitable right or interest. It does not revive against a later purchaser.

2.3 Investigation of title in unregistered land

Unlike registered land, the title in unregistered land can only be proven by title deeds. Therefore, before purchasing unregistered land the purchaser cannot check the title in a register but can do so by looking at the title deeds. The only register that the purchaser can search is the 'Land Charges Register' under the LCA 1971 as discussed in Section 2.2. In addition, 'overreaching' and the 'doctrine of notice' are going to apply. Based on these legal arrangements for unregistered land in England and Wales, the purchaser and/or their representative should carry out certain investigation and searches about the unregistered land. For this purpose, the following steps must be followed:

Step 1: Check the titles of the current seller of the land and those before him/her. You must check the title papers to establish a good root of title which must go back 15 years from the current date. Papers that you should check are **title deeds**, and the marriage and death certificates of the current and previous owners if there were any name changes.

Step 2: Check that the property description matches the plan. You should do this by comparing the property description in the title deeds and the property plan.

Step 3: Check if the property is subject to any **covenants** or **easements**. Covenants are restrictions imposed on the property such as you cannot run a business. Easements are rights granted to another person (neighbour) to use your land such as a right of way. In the example given in Figure 2.1, Noel has an easement (right of way) over Jemina's land. See Chapter 8 for further discussion. Also, you must inspect the property to see if you need any easements. If you do need one, you must ensure that they are granted expressly in a **deed**.

Step 4: Check all the owners' names to find out if the property is subject to any land charges. You can do this by searching the 'charges register' which is kept under the Land Charges Act 1972. It is important for you to note that this register is completely separate from the one kept for registered land.

Step 5: Once you have checked the charges register, please complete the purchase within 15 days from the date of search. This is because completion of the purchase within 15 days would give you the guarantee that you are not going to

21 *Wilkes v Spooner* [1911] 2 KB 473.

be bound by any new entries in the charges register made between the date of search and 15 days thereafter.

Step 6: Check that you have paid the appropriate stamp duties for purchasing the property. Stamp duty is set up by the government which can be fixed or variable depending on the value of the property.

Step 7: Finally, check that all documents including the transfer of title have been properly executed. You can do this by consulting a professional **conveyancer** who can check the documents against the regulation requirements such as the regulation of the Financial Conduct Authority or the Land Registry. Also, please check if the seller has discharged any outstanding mortgage. This can also be done by your conveyancer.

Chapter revision points

Existing priority interests in unregistered land: **Proprietary** interests in unregistered land can be split into the following four different groups:

(1) Legal rights (− 1).
(2) Equitable rights (+ 1) registrable under the LCA 1972.
(3) Equitable rights not registrable under the LCA 1972 because they are overreachable, e.g., **two trustees scenario**.
(4) Equitable rights which are neither registrable nor overreachable – where doctrine of notice is still applicable.

Please note the following general points on the issue of registration of rights as land charges:

- The definition of a purchaser will include a **mortgagee**.
- All unregistered land charges will remain enforceable if they are not void. We have seen that failure to register land charges makes them void against certain types of purchaser but if the person to whom the land is transferred is given the land as a gift or inherits it then, whether or not the right that should have been registered as land charge has been registered, it will bind the person to whom the land is transferred.
- All unregistered land charges remain enforceable against the person who granted them. Thus, in the example, Jemina was the person who gave Noel an equitable right of way. Therefore, he can insist on using that right of way while Jemina remains the owner, whether or not he has registered it as a land charge.
- In cases where a right could have been registered as a land charge, the doctrine of notice has NO application. This means if those rights could have been registered but were not actually registered as land charges then the doctrine of notice would not apply.

The 'doctrine of notice' applies to unregistered Land law. It protects a purchaser who did not have the knowledge of a third party's right or interest in the property from being bound by such right or interest. Therefore, you must inspect the property before purchasing it in order to find out if there is any hidden right or interest for which a purchaser may be bound.

You must also take a few key steps ranging from inspecting the property up to the completion of purchase. These steps include checking a good root of title for 15 years, searching for land charges, inspecting the property to find out any third-party rights or interests, checking the title deeds and property plan, easements, covenants, and paying the correct stamp duties.

Multiple choice question

1. Alan owns Green Gables (a large house with extensive grounds). He builds a cottage in part of the grounds and sells it to Bill in fee simple. In the conveyance to Bill in 2020 he imposes a restrictive covenant to prevent Bill from carrying on a business on the land. If Bill sells the cottage (unregistered land) to Cath, will she be bound by the covenant? Please choose TWO correct answers from the following options:
   (a) Cath will be bound by the covenant under the doctrine of notice even if the covenant has not been registered as a land charge.
   (b) Cath will be bound by the covenant if it is registered as a D (ii) land charge, and she has purchased a legal estate in the cottage.
   (c) Cath will be bound by the covenant even if she has purchased an equitable estate in the cottage.
   (d) Cath will not be bound by the covenant if she was unaware of the covenant.
   (e) Cath will not be bound by the covenant if it is registered in the wrong name, and she has searched against the correct name of the owners who owned the property for last 15 years.

Answer: See Appendix C.

2. In the above scenario, assume that Alan holds Green Gables on trust for his adult daughters, Ethel and Freda. If David buys Green Gables from Alan, will he be bound by the daughters' interests in the property? Select the CORRECT answer:
   (a) David will be bound because the doctrine of notice will automatically apply.
   (b) David will be bound as he has not overreached the beneficial interest of his daughters by making payment of the purchase price to at least two trustees.

(c) David will be bound if he is aware of the beneficial interest under the doctrine of notice as he has not overreached the beneficial interest of his daughters by making payment of the purchase price to at least two trustees.

(d) David will not be bound as the daughters' beneficial interests were not registered as land charges.

(e) David will not be bound as he was not aware of the daughters' beneficial interest in the cottage.

Answer: See Appendix C.

3 Registration of title (registered land)

Chapter overview

In Chapter 2, we discussed the issue of priority that applies to unregistered Land law. The LPA 1925, LCA 1972, and **common law** have dealt with the issues of priority to protect certain rights and interests which may bind a new purchaser of unregistered land. This legal framework also offers guidance for the new purchaser to investigate title so they can avoid responsibility to certain third-party rights and interests. This chapter also outlined the scope of application of the doctrine of notice. However, the unregistered system is becoming less important for two reasons, namely (a) as stated in Chapter 2, most land in England and Wales (over 87%) is now registered and the number is gradually going up, so only a small percentage of land is still unregistered; and (b) registration of title has become compulsory on sale and transfer of properties in England and Wales.[1]

In this chapter, we discuss the laws relating to the registration of title. The legal framework has evolved through fundamental changes made by the Land Registration Act 2002 (LRA 2002).[2] This legislation repealed its predecessor Land Registration Act 1925. It is very important for you to remember that the law of registered title land is very different from that of unregistered land. Whereas in the unregistered system a purchaser would require a vendor (seller) to show a good root of title (15 years) and hence a fresh investigation of title would be necessary on each sale, in the registered system the legal title would be investigated just once (by the Land Registrar) and then registered. Also, registration of title is the ultimate proof of title which means that a purchaser would only need to investigate the land register to find out what would be binding rather than undertaking the troublesome task of showing a good root of title for 15 years. As a result of this, a purchaser for value takes the legal estate subject to entries on the register and **overriding interests** but free from all other **estates** and interests whatsoever; s/he would not need to be concerned with rights and interests that are not protected on the register whether or not s/he has notice of them. At the end of this chapter, you shall be able to see how the system of registration of title has been designed to simplify **conveyancing**.

1 LRA 2002, S. 4, 27.
2 LRA 2002 came into force on 13 October 2003.

DOI: 10.4324/9781003204954-3

3.1 The basic concept of title registration

The aim of the registered land system was to ensure quick, efficient, and inexpensive transfer of estates and interests in the land while ensuring **third-party interests** were properly protected. The legal framework was designed to abolish the 'doctrine of notice' from the system of registered title land. The system is often described as being based on three principles:

- **The mirror principle**: The title register should reflect a complete and accurate record of the facts (rights and interests). However, there are cracks in the mirror, e.g., overriding interests.[3] 'Cracks in the mirror' will be discussed below.
- **The curtain principle**: The title register should be the sole and definitive source of information for proposed purchasers, but should not reveal sensitive information, e.g., beneficial interests under a trust. These interests are overreachable.[4] So like unregistered land, overreaching is available for registered land too.
- **The insurance principle**: The Land Registry will pay compensation to anyone who suffered a loss because of a defective title register. This might happen where the purchaser has suffered loss by relying on the information which was mistakenly or erroneously entered on the register.

3.1.1 Cracks in the mirror

The principle that the land register should reflect a complete and accurate record of the rights and interests in a registered title land (the mirror principle) has not materialised. This is because it is impractical and undesirable to enter absolutely everything in the land register. Also, registration of title is not intended to replace physical inspection of the land. Title registration exists to ease the purchaser's path, not to exclude his/her participation in the conveyancing process. Therefore, it is unlikely

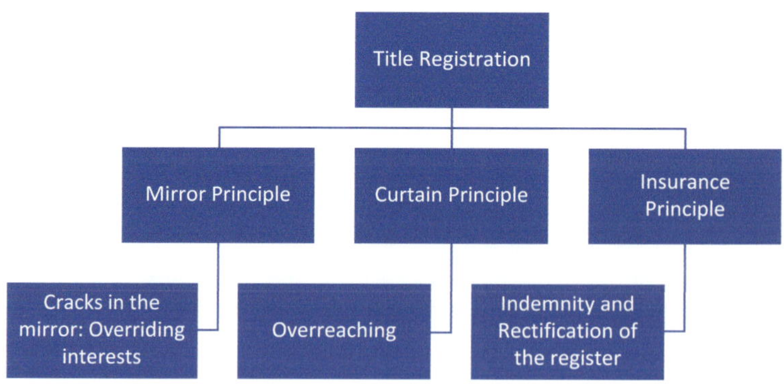

Figure 3.1 The key concept of title registration.

3 LRA 2002, Sch. 1 and 2.
4 LPA 1925, S. 27.

that the register will ever be a truly perfect mirror. For example, compulsory registration of a short lease of seven years or less, and rights created by **actual occupation**[5] is not required as this would not only overwhelm the records of the land register, but also impose a burden on the holders of these rights particularly where they are innocent and vulnerable. As the law must protect the vulnerable, certain rights and interests such as the short leases (seven years or less in length) and actual occupation remain as cracks in the mirror. These interests are also known as 'overriding interests'.

3.1.2 Overriding interests

Overriding interests are those interests that do not appear on the land register. A prudent purchaser needs to inspect the land and make enquiries so that s/he knows whether the land s/he is buying is affected by any overriding interests. These are a category of rights for which registration is strongly encouraged but is not compulsory. For instance, S. 71 LRA 2002 encourages a person making an application to register his/her title to disclose to the registrar any known overriding interests so that it may be entered on the land register [using Form DI]. There are **two categories** of overriding interests:

1. A broad category of interests which override on first registration of title (Schedule 1, LRA 2002), including leases of up to and including seven years, the property rights of people in occupation, easements, and **profits**.[6]
2. A shorter list of interests which override on the sale or transfer of land which is already registered (Schedule 3, LRA 2002), including leases of up to and including seven years, the property rights of people in occupation, easements, and profits, but with exceptions to rights of occupiers where the interests of those in the actual occupation are not readily discoverable because they are hidden.

Whether governed by Schedule 1 or Schedule 3, the rights of a person in actual occupation will override only to the extent that they **coincide** with that occupation. To further strengthen the mirror principle in the registered land, under Schedules 1 and 3 the rights of a person in actual occupation will not override a purchaser where either:

1. Enquiries have been made of the right-holder and s/he has failed to disclose the right in circumstances where he could reasonably be expected to disclose it (undiscovered): [Sch. 1 only].[7]

5 A person is in actual occupation where s/he holds a proprietary interest in the land which is protected by him/her by actually occupying the land as opposed to merely receiving rents and profits of the land per se: see *Strand Securities v Caswell* [1965]1 All ER 820; *Wishart v Credit and Mercantile [2015] EWCA Civ 655*.

6 For easements and profits, see Chapter 8.

7 *Williams and Glyn's Bank Ltd v Boland* [1980] 2 ALL ER 408.

2. The right-holder's actual occupation is not obvious on a reasonable inspection of the land, and the person potentially bound did not have actual knowledge of the interest at the time of the sale or transfer (undiscoverable): [Sch. 3 only].[8]

3.1.3 Overreaching

Like unregistered Land law, a beneficial interest held under a trust can be overreached by a purchaser paying the purchase-price to at least two trustees. This method of overreaching the beneficial interest under a trust was made available to registered Land law to make the sale and purchase of land held under a trust simple and straightforward. Under the curtain principle, the land register would disclose that a property is subject to a restriction, i.e., held under a trust. Therefore, a restriction is a form of entry that places limitations on the registered proprietor's powers of the land.[9] It prevents a sole legal owner (such a sole trustee) from selling or transferring the land to the potential detriment of the beneficial owner and deters potential buyers from buying the land until the restriction is removed. Please remember that if the overreaching does not occur the buyer of the land remains bound by the beneficial interests if those fall within the category of overriding interests. However, if they do not fall within the category of overriding interests a buyer of the registered title land takes it free of those interests but this does not apply to a non-purchaser for instance someone who received the property by gift or through succession.[10]

For a discussion about the functioning of the system of overreaching see Section 2.2 of Chapter 2. However, it is important to note that the LRA 2002 made provisions for entering third-party rights in the register in order to make it more mirror image like. Therefore, beneficial interests under a trust can be entered into the register by an entry as a notice.

3.1.4 Indemnity by the Land Registry

The land registry guarantees the accuracy of the entries in the land register and pledges to compensate those who suffer loss by relying on the register. For instance:

Jemina bought a house from Sandeep who had managed to register his name as the owner of the house by fraud. At the time of purchase, Jemina searched the land register and found Sandeep as the owner of the house. Based on this information Jemina bought the house from Sandeep. However, after a few months, Jemina found out that Sandeep defrauded Umar who never sold the house to him. Sandeep has absconded with the money. In these circumstances, both Jemina and Umar have been the victims of Sandeep's fraud. Jemina can

8 *Link Lending Ltd. v Bustard* [2010] EWCA Civ 424.
9 Land Registration Rules (LRR), Sch. 4.
10 LRA 2002, Ss. 28, 29.

claim indemnity as she relied on the land register. Also, Umar can make an application for rectification (correction) of the register so his name is restored in the register as the owner.[11] The ultimate result is that, while it is inevitable that Umar will lose the house but he will not be left financially out of pocket.[12]

3.2 Types of registers and their contents

The rights and interests in registered title land are listed in three types of registers namely, (a) the property register; (b) the proprietorship register; and (c) the charges register. The contents of these registers are outlined below:

A: Property register
This gives:

- A description of the property.
- The date the property was first registered.
- Any rights it may benefit from, such as an easement.
- If the property is **leasehold**, the register may also show details of the lease, such as the date, the parties, and its length.
- Details of entry of legal rights under S. 1 LPA 1925 such as a freehold, or lease that has more than seven years to expire.

B: Proprietorship register
This shows:

- The name and address of the current owner.
- When they bought the property.
- How much they paid for it (if sold since 1 April 2000).
- Any restrictions that limit the power of the owner, for example, to stop them from securing a loan without their mortgage lender's consent.
- The class of the title, such as an '**absolute title**' or '**possessory title**', which reflects the level of guarantee (based on the strength of evidence given).[13]

C: Charges register
Information in the charges register may include:

- Mortgages or other financial burdens secured on the property (though this won't show the amount of money involved).
- Rights or interests that limit how the land or property can be used, such as leases, easements, or covenants.

11 LRA 2002, Sch. 8.
12 *Bakrania v Lloyds Bank* [2017] UK FTT (PC).
13 LRA 2002, S. 2, 3, 4, and 27.

3.3 Interests protectable by registration

The following interests are protectable by registration. That means they must be protected by registration:

- **Fee simple** (also known as freehold land).
- Leases with over seven years left to run.
- Expressly created easements where the **servient** (burdened) land has registered title.
- Expressly created profits.

In addition to the above, certain third-party rights should be protected by an entry in the land register. That means, these rights can only be entered on the register as opposed to registration. These are equitable interests in another person's land. These include all interests which are neither registerable nor overriding (*may also be overriding*). There are two types of interests:

1. Those interests that would be registrable under the LCA in unregistered land (**notice**): These are **third-party interests** in unregistered land which would be registerable under the LCA, which bind a purchaser if protected by an entry in the land register; if they are not protected, they do not bind a new purchaser even if s/he has had notice. For instance, an estate contract (contract to sell and buy land) is registerable under the LCA so if it is not entered in the land register as a notice then the buyer is not going to be bound by the estate contract even if s/he has had knowledge about that.
2. The interests of beneficiaries under a trust which can be protected by an entry of a **restriction**: these are interests of beneficiaries under a trust which are capable of being overreached. Of course, if a sale or transfer of land is made without valuable **consideration**, the transferee (purchaser) takes subject to all pre-existing property rights, irrespective of whether they are registered or overriding.[14] For instance, interests under a trust are not capable of protection in the land register under the LRA 2002. Instead, a restriction may be entered to facilitate overreaching by informing a potential buyer of the land. But it is important for you to note that the entry of a restriction does not protect an equitable interest and no notice for such interest may be entered.

These two types of interests must be registered against the land they burden NOT against the owner of the land.[15] Failure to register these interests may mean that they lose their priority against any registered purchaser UNLESS they fall within the category of overriding interests under **Sch. 1 or 3** LRA 2002 (actual occupation, short

14 LRA 2002, S. 28.

15 Please remember this is not like registration of land charges in respect to unregistered land where the charges must be registered against the name of the landowner. See Chapter 2.

leases for seven years or less, legal easements, and profits).[16] These interests are entered in the land register of title (this is not the charges register as in for unregistered land) of the burdened land by means of a **NOTICE** or **RESTRICTION**.[17] If not entered in the register in this way then they are valid against non-purchaser, such as a person who received the property by gift or through succession.[18] Examples of these types of interests are contract for sale, covenants, **option to purchase**, **proprietary estoppel**, leases granted for seven years or less, and easements.

Please note that, while a restriction, such as conditions to fulfil to overreach the beneficial interest under a trust, is entered in the proprietorship register, a notice is entered in the charges register. An application for entering a restriction in the register must be supported by documentary evidence. For this purpose, the registrar will need to verify the title that is being applied for entering into the register before the actual entry. For instance, the applicant must prove that s/he is in actual occupation before their **possessory title** (such as actual occupation) can be entered in the register.[19] If there is no evidence submitted with the application, and/or if the current landowner refused to give consent to it, the type of notice that will be entered in the register is a '**unilateral notice'** as opposed to an '**agreed notice**'. These two

Table 3.1 Agreed and unilateral notice

Agreed notice	Unilateral notice
• The registrar may enter an agreed notice where: ○ (a) the applicant himself is a registered proprietor entitled to be registered as such; or ○ (b) those in (a) consents; or ○ (c) the registrar is satisfied with the validity of the claim: S. 34 LRA 2002. • **Example**: 'Home right' under Family Law Act 1996, inheritance tax liability, **customary right**, **public right**, variation of a lease under S. 38 Landlord and Tenant Act 1987.	• As opposed to agreed notice, a 'unilateral notice' is entered without consent from the current landowner. However, evidence is required to submit an application to HM Land Registry. • The Land Registry gives notice to the proprietor of the land to challenge. • Unlike agreed notice, a unilateral notice will also identify the person entitled to the right under the Notice.

16 LRA 2002, S. 11, 12, 29, and 30.
17 LRA 2002, S. 32 (1).
18 LRA 2002, S. 28.
19 LRA, S. 9 (5), 10 (6).

types of notice, which are both capable of being entered in the register, are outlined in Table 3.1.

3.4 Basic and special priority rules

It is important for you to note that land must be registered within two months of the completion of purchase. If a transferee (buyer) fails to register within two months, s/he will only have an equitable title in the land and could be vulnerable to a subsequent fraudulent sale of the land in the name of the person from whom s/he bought it. However, please note that overriding interests such as persons in actual occupation, short leases for seven years or less, and impliedly created easements, are not subject to any vulnerability due to delayed registration (Sch. 3, para 2 LRA 2002). Also, you must remember the following basic and special rule in relation to a transfer of registered land:

- **Basic rule:** The transferee, who is not a purchaser, is bound by all pre-existing proprietary interests: S. 28 LRA 2002.[20]
- **Special rule**: A purchaser has priority over all interests except those entered on the register and those overriding within Schedule 3: S. 29 LRA 2002.

Chapter revision points

- Whereas in the unregistered system a purchaser will require a seller to show a good root of title, in the registered system the legal title is investigated just once (by the Land Registrar) and then registered.
- Unlike unregistered title land, the doctrine of notice has no application in registered land.
- The primary aim of the registered land system is to ensure quick, efficient, and inexpensive transfer of estates and interests in land while ensuring third-party interests are properly protected.
  - This aim is being pursued by adopting the three key principles namely, the mirror principle, the curtain principle, and the insurance principle.
- However, it is very important for you to note that there are cracks in the mirror which may not be discoverable by searching the land register, e.g., short lease, overriding interests, legal easements, and profits. Therefore, the land register is not yet an accurate reflection of the rights and interests that can exist in a land.
- Overriding interests are dangerous for the purchaser of a registered title because these are hidden interests on land which can be binding on a buyer even after purchasing a title to land.

20 See *Halifax v Popeck [2008] All ER 281;* and *Gold Harp v Macleod [2014] EWCA Civ 532.*

- A person may choose to register title to their land voluntarily as this will give the insurance that their title is guaranteed by the fact of registration.

Multiple choice questions

1. Wendy lives in Wren Cottage, the matrimonial home, of which her husband, Habib, was the registered proprietor with absolute title. In 2021, Habib deserted Wendy and mortgaged the cottage to a bank. The mortgage payments were well in arrears and the bank seek possession of the cottage. Wendy, who gave Habib £10,000 towards the purchase-price of the cottage, refuses to leave. Which of the following options are CORRECT?
   (a) Wendy cannot refuse to leave because she is not a registered proprietor of Wren cottage.
   (b) Wendy cannot refuse to leave because the Bank has a legal interest in the cottage.
   (c) Wendy can refuse to leave the cottage if she has an overriding interest by actual occupation and she has entered that interest as a notice in the land register.
   (d) Wendy can refuse to leave if she can establish an overriding interest by actual occupation and she does not need to enter this into the land register as a notice.
   (e) Wendy can refuse to leave because the bank is a mortgagee but not a purchaser, so they do not have priority over her interest in the cottage.

Answer: See Appendix C.

2. Which of the following statements are correct:
   (a) A purchaser of land by fraud is bound by any equitable interests occurring prior to that purchase, as the transaction was not made by valuable consideration.
   (b) A purchaser of land by fraud is not bound by any equitable interests occurred prior to that purchase, as the transaction was not made by valuable consideration.
   (c) A purchaser has priority over all interests except those entered on the register and those overriding within Schedule 3.
   (d) A court or registrar can decide the priority of a purchaser against the basic and special priority rules, if doing that would give the party the priority which it should have had but for the mistake.
   (e) A victim of fraud cannot claim any indemnity from the Land Registry because s/he is not protected from fraudulent entry in the register.

Answer: See Appendix C.

4 Co-ownership 1

Informal acquisition of title (implied trusts)

Chapter overview

Co-ownership occurs when two or more people are entitled to simultaneous or concurrent enjoyment of a land. This situation occurs frequently in everyday life. For example:

- When a married couple purchases a matrimonial home.
- When a person dies leaving the house to her three children in equal shares.

When a land is owned by co-owners, the most important question is – 'what is the proportion of their ownership?' This is decided by a set of legal principles known as '**joint tenancy**' and '**tenancy in common**'. In a '**joint tenancy**' the shares of the parties are not defined, but in a '**tenancy in common**' it is so defined.

This chapter discusses a very common co-ownership scenario that may occur informally between the parties. In this scenario, the parties create the legal relationship impliedly, and in most instances without knowing or thinking about the legal implications of their relationship. For instance, married or unmarried couples often buy properties together without even knowing or thinking about the possible legal consequences of their family home if the relationship breaks down the line. Because the parties do not expressly enter into a legal relationship, this situation is known as an implied trust. Thus, in an implied trust situation, two parties become owner of a property where either or both of their names appear in the land register as owners. This situation creates an implied trust by operation of law. This chapter discusses the legal mechanism for creating this type of trust and how the law applies to co-owners in this situation.

4.1 Joint tenancy and tenancy in common

Co-owners may be **joint tenants** or **tenants in common**. Only a joint tenancy can exist at law, but in **equity** it is also possible for either joint tenancy or tenancy in common to exist, and for co-ownership to arise informally (even by conduct without the parties realising the implications of their behaviour).

DOI: 10.4324/9781003204954-4

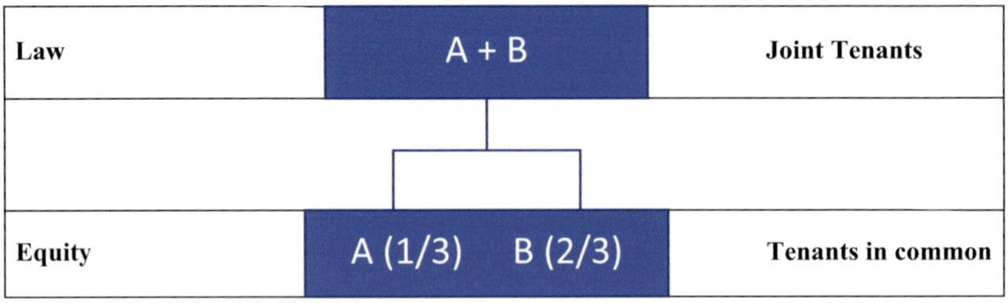

Figure 4.1 Legal and equitable positions in co-ownership.

Under a joint tenancy, all owners are entitled to the entire property; none has any specific or identified *'share'*. For instance, where two joint tenants bought a property but only one of them was registered as an owner (sole name case). Many family homes are held by couples as joint tenants both in law and in equity because the size of their shares was not decided at the time of purchase. For instance, where a couple bought a family home in their joint names (joint name cases) but without deciding the size of their shares. The right of **survivorship** applies to joint tenants but not to tenants in common which means that if a joint tenant dies his/her right passes to the remaining joint tenants. A **joint tenancy** cannot pass under a will or succession. However, if a joint tenant wants to make a will or transfer his or her portion of the property then s/he will have to formally split his/her portion by following a certain legal process known as **severance**.[1] For instance, in the following diagram (Figure 4.1) where A and B bought a house together they could either be joint tenants where their respective size of shares is not determined, or they could be tenants in common (in **equity**) where their respective size of shares is determined, i.e., A1/3 and B2/3.

Where a land is held under tenancy in common, each owner has an identifiable *'undivided share'* which s/he can sell, transfer, leave by will, etc. This means that the owners know the size of their shares but do not know which part of the property they own. For instance, the co-owners know that they each own 50% of the property but they do not know whether that 50% is from the east or west side of the land. It is very important for you to note that the right of survivorship does not apply to tenants in common.

4.2 Trusts in a family home

A trust in a family home is very common in England and Wales. This occurs when a married couple bought a matrimonial home, or an unmarried couple bought a house to live together. In these situations, the property was purchased by the parties jointly but either one or both of their names appeared on the land register. Whereas the law treats both of them as co-owners, the extent of their legal right in the property

1 Severance is discussed in Chapter 5.

depends on the nature of the **implied trust** created by the transaction. In other words, the application of the law depends on whether the co-ownership is under sole name or joint name.

4.2.1 Resulting trusts

A **resulting trust** occurs when a person contributes *directly towards the purchase price* of a land but does not have his or her name on the legal title (known as 'purchase in the name of another'). In such a case there will be a *presumption* that the contributor has a beneficial interest in the land behind a resulting trust. A **resulting trust** generates *shares in proportion* to what is paid towards the purchase price. For instance, Fahim and Joya were an unmarried couple. They bought a property where Fahim paid 40% and Joya paid 60% of the purchase price. Only Fahim's name appeared as the registered proprietor (a sole name case). They did not decide the size of their shares in the property at the time of purchase. In this situation, the law will presume that Fahim is the legal owner who is holding the property in a **resulting trust** for the benefit of himself and Joya. This is a resulting trust scenario where the size of their shares in the property will be determined according to what they have paid. This would include any payments towards the deposit. Thus, in order to create a resulting trust, the following conditions must satisfy:

1. There must be evidence of express discussion between the parties that the property is to be shared beneficially between the parties even if only one of them has been the **registered proprietor**.
2. In the absence of such evidence, the court would only infer a common intention where a person (who is not the legal owner) has made direct contributions to the purchase price.[2]

In our above example, it is very likely that Fahim's share in the property is 40% and Joya's share is 60% where Fahim is a legal owner who is holding the property in a **resulting trust** for himself and Joya. The conclusion is based on point (b), there is no evidence of express discussion so the application of resulting trust can be inferred from Joya's direct contribution towards the purchase price. However, the current law is that in the absence of an express discussion between the parties the court will take into account 'the whole course of conduct between the parties' in determining not only what would be a fair share but also what would be the nature of their interest in the property'. Please see the following section for a detailed discussion about this development of the law by the jurisprudence and case law of the Judiciary of England and Wales.

2 *Lloyds Bank v Rosset* [1991] 1 AC 107.

4.2.2 Common intention constructive trusts

A constructive trust occurs where a person has contributed, directly or indirectly, to the price or value of the land (home) and there was a 'common intention' or express agreement between the parties that he or she should have a share in its ownership; or where such common intention can be proven, in addition to an 'excuse' or lie from the legal owner as to why the land was not being conveyed into joint names. A constructive trust generates *according to what is fair in all the circumstances*. Therefore, the key features of a **constructive trust**, which stands out from a **resulting trust**, are (a) direct or indirect contribution to the purchase price; and (b) common intention between the parties about their shares in the property. Whereas direct payment to the purchase price includes payment towards the deposit, indirect payment includes mortgages, bills, repairs, and other household expenditures such as childcare expenses. Therefore, in a **constructive trust**, the parties' indirect contribution as well as direct contribution towards the purchase price are considered. In addition to this, a common intention or express agreement must be present or could be proved. But mere excuse or lie from the legal owner as to 'why the property was not conveyed in their joint names' would not suffice to prove common intention. Rather, more cogent evidence is necessary.

For instance, in the example given in Section 4.2.1 between Fahim and Joya, the transaction can be a common intention **constructive trust** if the parties have agreed that they would have an equal share in the property and they will contribute equally to the mortgage and other expenditures. This is irrespective of the fact that the property was registered under Fahim's name only because Joya's business was not doing very well so they both thought that including Joya's name in the land register would be a huge risk (from potential creditors) of losing the property if her business suffers losses or she becomes bankrupt.

An important question arises when there is no evidence to suggest what the parties had expressly agreed or intended about their respective size of shares of the property, but they contributed directly to the purchase price. Should the court prefer a **resulting trust** in this situation? The current jurisprudence and case law suggest that the court is going to take into account 'the whole course of conduct between the parties in determining what would be a fair share'.[3] They also suggest that payment of money alone will not give rise to an equitable interest in the property and there must be an agreement or understanding between the parties that the payer should have an interest.[4] The rationale behind this position is that one party may have received money from another as a gift or loan. This legal position

3 *Oxley* v *Hiscock* [2004] EWCA Civ 546.
4 *Lightfoot* v *Lightfoot-Brown* [2005] EWCA Civ 201.

emphasises the necessity to have an express agreement or understanding in order to create a **constructive trust**. However, this situation has given rise to the question – 'is it fair to deny a constructive trust in the absence of an express agreement or understanding?' The judiciary in England and Wales were facing this question very often where there was no sufficient evidence to suggest that the parties had expressly agreed or had a common understanding about the nature of their (one of their) interest in the property that they purchased. The judiciary started to lean towards finding a constructive trust from 'the whole course of conduct between the parties' in determining not only what would be a fair share but also what would be the nature of their interest in the property'.[5] Therefore, the current law does not require the parties to establish a common intention or express agreement in order to imply a **constructive trust**.[6]

In summary, under the current law if there is an express agreement between the parties the court is likely to respect that unless there is a good reason for not doing that. In the absence of an express agreement, the court will take into account the whole course of dealing between the parties. There are situations where the court found good reasons for not taking into account an express agreement between the parties. For instance, when the parties agreed to keep a **joint tenancy** which only existed in law. In this situation, it may be unconscionable for any dependent children if the court applies the parties' intention. This is because a **joint tenancy** in law cannot be severed so giving effect to the parties' intention, which is to keep the property as a **joint tenancy** in law, is likely to deprive those children from the property due to the application of the **survivorship** principle.[7] For instance, if the parties wanted to own a matrimonial home under a **joint tenancy** in law then if the parent with whom the children are living dies the other parent will become the sole owner by survivorship. This will eventually deprive the children from the house. In cases like this where the court cannot give effect to the party's common intention, which can also change in the course of time, the court can impute the intention on the parties. This is because the **beneficial interest** cannot be inferred in a situation where the parties' common intention changes in the course of time. This is very common in joint name cases, i.e., where the property is registered in the joint names of the parties.

4.2.1.1 Joint name cases

Where two or more people purchase a family home in their joint names, the law presumes that they intend to own the property as **joint tenants** in both law and **equity**. The presumption may be rebutted by evidence that it was not so intended, or the intention had changed in the course of time. If the presumption is rebutted or

5 *Crossley* v *Crossley* [2005] EWCA Civ 1581.
6 *Stack* v *Dowden* [2007] UKHL 17.
7 *Jones v Kernott* [2011] UKSC 53.

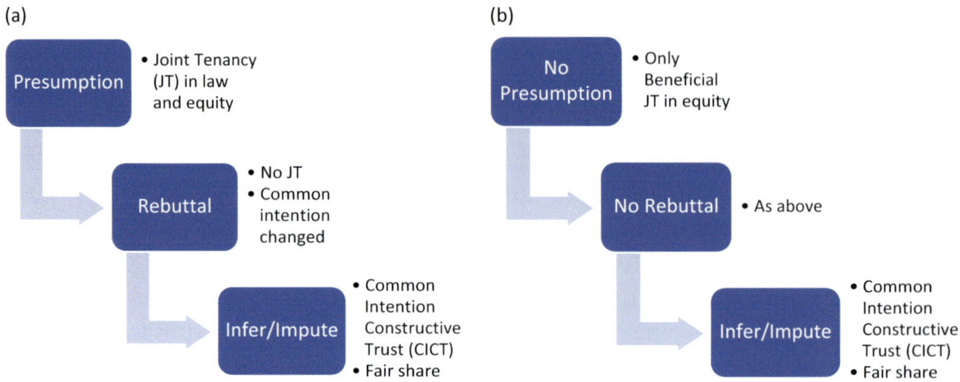

Figure 4.2 (a) Process in joint name cases. (b) Process in sole name cases.

the intention has changed the court can either draw an inference from the course of dealing between the parties or it can impute an intention instead where inference is not possible. As a result, the court may have to impute an intention to the parties which they never have had.

4.2.1.2 Sole name cases

Sole name cases (where the property is bought in the name of one party only) are problematic. Due to lack of a **declaration of trust**, a sole legal owner cannot hold a beneficial **joint tenancy** in law. As a result, sole name cases are co-ownerships under a **joint tenancy** in **equity**. In this situation, on the one hand the party whose name is not in the proprietorship register has to establish a common intention constructive trust, and on the other hand the party whose name is in the register can only admit (in the absence of an express agreement or **resulting trust**) a beneficial joint tenancy in **equity**. Thus, **equity** will have to decide the existence of a common intention **constructive trust** in the absence of an express agreement. Unlike joint name cases, the court cannot presume a beneficial joint tenancy but can infer or impute a **constructive trust** based on the course of dealings between the parties.[8]

It is important for you to note that, the reason for the case law that developed certain process for inferring or imputing common intention **constructive trust** in sole name and joint name cases is that there are a lack of legislative provisions in this regard. Hence, the judges have been able to exercise their discretion in these cases. This situation has given the judges to infer or impute based on financial contribution but there is no set guidance for the judges as to how they should do this.

8 *Aspden v Elvy* [2012] EWHC 1387 (Ch).

4.3 Intersection with proprietary estoppel?

You will come across the issue – whether to argue a **constructive trust** or **proprietary estoppel** in an **implied trust** situation. A **proprietary estoppel** creates an implied right in a property where the owner promised someone that the latter would have a right in the property if they did do or not do certain things, and they followed that condition. For instance, the owner of a farm promised to his niece that the latter would have a right in the farm if she left her current job and moved into the farmhouse to look after the farm. In this situation, the niece can make a claim under '**proprietary estoppel**' if the farm owner did not keep his promise**. Constructive trust** has been discussed above in this chapter already.

Whereas arguments for both **constructive trust** and **proprietary estoppel** (PE) are convincing and powerful, it is very important for you to understand what the client wants. It does not depend on whether the parties are married couples or cohabitees or just relatives. If the client is looking to have a fair share in the property in question based on his/her course of dealings with the other co-owner/s, it may be better to argue **constructive trust**. This is because the court is likely to take into account the course of dealings between the parties in absence of any proof to show an express agreement, which is a requirement for **proprietary estoppel**. On the contrary, if the client is looking to get a lump sum (money back) that they invested in a property rather than only an interest then it may be better to argue PE. For instance, where parents or grandparents moved into a property and spent a lot of money to build an extension or refurbish a room. This is because in a claim for **proprietary estoppel** the contribution is likely to substantially add to the value of the property. However, it is important for you to note that the legal requirements to satisfy a proprietary estoppel are very cumbersome. The court will only intervene if three requirements are fulfilled, namely (a) a representation made or assurance given to the Claimant; (b) reliance by the Claimant on the representation or assurance; and (c) some detriment incurred by the Claimant as a consequence of that reliance.[9] Whereas these elements would always be necessary but might, in a particular case, not be sufficient. Thus, for example, the representation or assurance would need to be sufficiently clear and unequivocal; the reliance by the Claimant would need to be reasonable in all the circumstances; and the detriment would need to be sufficiently substantial to justify the intervention of equity. Therefore, it is very important that a lawyer must consider the available evidence very carefully before making an argument for either **constructive trust** or PE. It is also very important for you to note that, after analysing the financial contribution it might appear to a judge that the outcome would be the same. However, depending on the facts and available evidence a lawyer should consider both **constructive trust** and PE. And, after careful consideration they should put forward the most suitable grounds for their clients.

9 Proprietary estoppel is discussed in Chapter 7.

Chapter revision points

- A **co-ownership** is where two or more people are entitled to the simultaneous/concurrent enjoyment of a land.
- A co-ownership can be either a **joint tenancy** in law or a **tenancy in common** in equity. It is also possible for a **joint tenancy** to exist in equity.
- The most common scenario for impliedly created **co-ownership** is a trust in a family home. Trust in a family home can be either **resulting trust** or common intention **constructive trust**. However, the current law favours common intention **constructive trust** in the absence of an express agreement between the parties.
- In a common intention **constructive trust** (CICT), the court takes into account the whole course of dealing between the parties.
- In a CICT situation the court's approach differ based on whether it is a sole name or joint name case. Whereas in a sole name case the only possibility is a beneficial **joint tenancy**, in a joint name case a rebuttable presumption exists for a **joint tenancy** in law and **equity**. Once the court determines the applicable position, it can infer or impute a CICT and a fair share between the parties.
- Both CICT and **proprietary estoppel** (PE) can be argued in impliedly created co-ownership cases. However, depending on what the client is looking for, a lawyer should consider the evidence available to decide whether to argue CICT or PE or both. It is possible that the outcome of a case would be the same irrespective of applying CICT or PE. In that situation, the court is expected to give its reasoning for adopting either CICT or PE or both.

Multiple choice question

Sarah lives in Green Cottage, a matrimonial home, of which both she and her husband, Brian, are the registered proprietors. They each paid half of the deposit. Brian paid the monthly mortgage payments and Sarah paid the household bills. The relationship broke down in 2021. They both wanted to sell the cottage. Which one of the following is INCORRECT?

(a) The law presumes that both Brian and Sarah are joint tenants in law and equity.
(b) The presumption that both Brian and Sarah are joint tenants in law and equity is rebuttable.
(c) In the absence of a common intention, the court can infer a fair share between the co-owners.

(d) In the absence of a common intention and where an inference is impossible or unconscionable, the court can impute a fair share between the co-owners.
(e) The court can allocate shares according to the contribution of co-owners in the purchase price.

Answer: See Appendix C.

5 Co-ownership 2

Trusts of land

Chapter overview

In the previous chapter, we discussed the creation of common intention **constructive trust** in a **co-ownership** setting when a married or unmarried couple bought property but without specifying the size of their shares at the time of buying. We have seen that the legal position has been changed by the court in recent years. The current law considers a common intention between the parties but if there is no common intention the court can infer or impute one in order to allocate a fair share between the parties.

In this chapter, we discuss another co-ownership situation where parties may or may not be in a relationship and they buy a property together without specifying the size of their shares. This is a common situation when friends and/or siblings buy a property together. We also discuss the implication of the Trusts of Land and Appointment of Trustees Act 1996 (TOLATA) to regulate the rights and duties of the **trustees** and **beneficiaries**. The **trustees** are legal owners of a piece of land whose names appear in the **land register** as **registered proprietors**. Conversely, the **beneficiaries** are not legal owners, but they only receive benefits from the property held by the **trustees**. This relationship between the **trustee** and **beneficiaries** is known as 'trusts of land'. People create **trusts** in situations such as where the beneficiaries themselves cannot be the legal owners because they are under 18, or because the creator of the trust does not want any spendthrift **beneficiaries** to take control of the trust property as a legal owner so the latter cannot sell the property for money to spend in luxury, or reckless investment, or gambling.

5.1 The methods of creating co-ownership

In the previous chapter, we discussed **joint tenancy** and **tenancy in common**. In a joint tenancy the parties' size of shares is not decided at the time of purchase of a property by the **co-owners**. However, in a **tenancy in common** the size of shares is allocated at the time of purchase or later on by the parties. Please note that the process by which a **joint tenancy** can become a **tenancy in common** is known as **Severance**. The implication of severance is that once a property becomes a **tenancy in common** the **co-owners** have a defined share in the property so they can sell their

DOI: 10.4324/9781003204954-5

shares, pass it to their successors, or leave it in a **will**. However, they cannot do these (sell or leave the property in a **will**) unless their property turns into a **tenancy in common**. Please also note that law only recognises a **joint tenancy**, but **equity** recognises both a **joint tenancy** and **tenancy in common**.[1] Another key important reason for you to know whether a property is a **joint tenancy** or **tenancy in common** is that the doctrine of '**survivorship**' applies to **joint tenancy** but not to a **tenancy in common**. As a result, in a **joint tenancy** if one of the co-owners dies his/her interest in the property passes on to the remaining surviving co-owners.

For instance, Julia and James bought a house together in 2020 but they did not decide the size of their shares. So, the house was under a joint tenancy in law. In 2021, James died without severing his share in the house. As a result, the house remained as a joint tenancy and James's share in the house would pass on to Julia according to the doctrine of survivorship. Thus, Julia would become the sole owner of the house which would no longer be under co-ownership.

It is very important for you to remember that law only recognises up to four co-owners in a property under a **joint tenancy**.[2] So, if a property has more than four co-owners then the first four of them will be recognised as legal owners under a **joint tenancy** and the rest of the co-owners will only be recognised as **equitable** owners under a **joint tenancy**.

For instance, Abraham (30), Bianca (28), Charlotte (25), David (22), and Emily (17) bought a house together. In this situation, only Abraham, Bianca, Charlotte, and David are legal owners in a joint tenancy. But Emily is only an owner in equity and the rest of the co-owners hold the house in trust for themselves and Emily. The reasons for which Emily cannot be a legal owner are: (a) Only the first four co-owners can be legal owners; and (b) a co-owner will have to be at his/her age of majority, i.e., 18 years old in order to hold a legal title.[3]

5.1.1 Joint tenancy and the four unities

The existence of a **joint tenancy** begs the question 'are the four unities present?' If not, there cannot be a **joint tenancy** (in both law and equity). It is important for you

1 Please see Figure 4.1 and adjacent discussion to understand more about the functionality of a joint tenancy and a tenancy in common.

2 Trustee Act 1925, S. 34.

3 LPA 1925, S. 1(6).

to note that these four unities are the key elements for a **joint tenancy** to exist so all four of them must be present.

- **Unity of title** requires that all co-owners derive their interests from the same document or act. For instance, the same title document must be used to buy a property for the co-owners. However, **leasehold** title is an exception to this rule because leaseholders may sign separate agreements.
- **Unity of time** requires that the interests of all co-owners vest in them at the same time. So, each co-owner must buy the property at the same time. If a co-owner joins later in the **co-ownership**, then that person cannot be a **joint tenant**.
- **Unity of interest** requires that all co-owners have the same interest in the land meaning that each co-owner must have the same type of interest in the land. For instance, if they buy a **freehold title** then all co-owners must have a freehold title in the land. It would not suffice if a few of them have freehold titles and the rest of them have **leasehold titles**, which is a different type of interest in land.
- **Unity of possession** requires that each co-owner is as much entitled to possession of the land as any other co-owner. This means that each co-owner is entitled to possession of the property and one of them cannot exclude or restrict the others' right of possession.

Based on the above, co-owners cannot claim **joint tenancy** on two separate properties at the same time because of the lack of a unity of title. In situations like this, the co-owners do not derive their interests from the same document or act. However, there is an exception to this rule. For instance, a joint tenancy is possible in separate properties where two or more business partners buy two or more pieces of land as part of their partnership assets. Also, where two or more partners acquire two or more pieces of land for their several business purposes in the partnership.

It is very important for you to remember that only if all four unities are present there can be a **joint tenancy**. But a **tenancy in common** requires **only unity of possession** to be shown. However, other unity (e.g. unity of time) might also be present. For instance, a **tenancy in common** may exist where the co-owners purchased a property at the same time but one of them only has a life interest which only exists as long as that person is alive, and the rest of the co-owners have absolute interests in the property. In this setting, although the unities of possession and time of each co-owner exist the unity of title and interest do not. As a result, the property is under a **tenancy in common**.

5.2 Severance

Severance is the process by which a **joint tenancy** in **equity** can convert into a **tenancy in common** in **equity**, thus destroying survivorship in equity. As stated above, only **joint tenancy** is possible at law, hence severance is not possible for the legal title. Therefore, severance is only possible in **equity** to convert a **joint tenancy** into a **tenancy in common**. However, there are six ways in which a **joint tenancy** may be severed.[4]

1. **Alienation *inter vivos***: This (e.g., where Xavier and Young are joint tenants and Young sells his interest to Paul) will sever Young's interest by **destroying unity of title**. Where a joint tenant becomes bankrupt and his property becomes compulsorily vested in his **trustee in bankruptcy**, this will also sever the joint tenancy.
2. **Acquisition of a different interest in the land**: Where Alan and Suzie are joint tenants for life and Suzie acquires a **freehold** interest in the land. This attacks the unity of interest.
3. **Mutual agreement**: A mutual agreement to sever, or to deal with the land in a manner which implies severance. It is important for you to note that a valid contract concerning land is required to be in writing.[5]
4. **Course of dealing**: Course of dealing is sufficient to indicate a **common intention** that one of the joint tenants should be regarded as having an undivided share. There are a few successful examples of this.[6] The most common example is, if one of the co-owners wants to move out of the property by offering to sell it and one of the other co-owners agrees to buy that share, and they have concluded a contract in writing.
5. **Notice in writing**: A joint tenant can sever his/her joint tenancy by giving notice in writing of his/her intention to do so to all other joint tenants.[7]
6. **Homicide**: This unusual form of severance operates because a joint tenant who kills another joint tenant will not be allowed to profit from his crime, and so survivorship must not operate.[8] It is important for you to note that, in case of an 'involuntary manslaughter' where one co-owner killed another co-owner by accident, the **joint tenancy** may not sever.

5.3 Trusts of Land and Appointment of Trustees Act (TOLATA) 1996

TOLATA came into force on 1 January 1997. From this date, a **trustee** is not under a duty to sell a property held on **trust**.[9] As a result, the **beneficiaries**' interests are better protected under TOLATA. Therefore, a beneficiary's interest must be **overreached** by making payment to two trustees in case of non-commercial property.[10] Also, a **trustee** will have to consult the **beneficiary** or even obtain the latter's consent

4 *Williams v Hensman* (1861) 70 E.R. 862.
5 Law of Property (Miscellaneous Provisions) Act 1989, S. 2.
6 *Gore and Snell v Carpenter* (1990) 60 P & CR 456, ChD.
7 LPA 1925 S. 36 (2); see also *Harris v Goddard* [1983] 1 WLR 1203, CA.
8 *Re K* [1985] Ch 85.
9 TOLATA 1996, S. 4 and 5.
10 Overreaching is discussed in Chapter 2 and 3.

before selling or dealing with the property in any other way such as investment or improvement of the property. The beneficiaries also have a general right to occupy the property which prevents the **trustee** from selling the property against the former's permission or consent.[11]

Under TOLATA, the trustees have broader powers. For instance, they can now delegate any of their powers to a beneficiary of full age, i.e., over 18 years old.[12] However, if there is any dispute about the exercise of the trustee's powers and functions, either the **trustee** or the **beneficiary** can apply for a court order to resolve that.[13] The court has also a greater scope to consider a dispute between a **trustee** and **beneficiary** in a hearing. For instance, the court can consider the following in an application for an order:

- The intentions of the creator of the trust.
- The purposes of the trust.
- The welfare of any minor whose home is in the property.
- The interests of any secured creditor, e.g., mortgagee.[14]

The above shows that, under TOLATA 1996 the court has the power to consider not only the intention of the creator of a **trust** or the purpose of it but also the interest of any minor as well as any secured creditor.

Chapter revision points

- Since 1 January 1926 (when the LPA 1925 came into force), co-ownership is either **joint tenancy** or **tenancy in common**.
- Law only recognises four co-owners in a property, and these are also the maximum number of people who can be **trustees**.
- Severance is the process by which a **joint tenancy** in **equity** can convert into a **tenancy in common** in **equity**, thus destroying survivorship in **equity**.
- A key question to ask concerning severance is: are there any words of severance in the grant indicating that the tenants were to take as tenants in common (e.g., X and Y in equal shares stated in a **will**)?
- Remember that only **joint tenancy** is possible at law, hence severance is not possible for the legal title. So, you need to follow the severance process in equity.
- There are six ways in which a **joint tenancy** may be severed (i.e., convert into a tenancy in common) such as alienation *inter vivos* (selling his/her interest

11 TOLATA 1993, Ss. 12, and 13.
12 TOLATA 1996, Ss. 6–9.
13 TOLATA 1993, S. 14.
14 TOLATA 1993, S. 15; see also *Begum v Hafiz* [2015] EWCA Civ 801.

by a joint tenant in his/her lifetime), acquisition of a different interest in the land, mutual agreement, course of dealing, notice in writing, and homicide.

- TOLATA 1996 have changed the law in relation to the duties of trustees and rights of the beneficiaries. This legislation requires trustees to consult or even obtain consent before dealing with a trust property. It also gives trustees the power to delegate their function to a full age **beneficiary**. Additionally, the court has now broader jurisdiction to address issues or disagreements between a **trustee** and **beneficiary**.

Multiple choice questions

1. Abu dies leaving his property in a will in joint names of Bevan (24) and Christy (22). The will does not say what shares they are given. Which of the following is CORRECT?
   (a) The property is held by Bevan and Christy as joint tenants.
   (b) The property is held by Bevan and Christy as tenants in common.
   (c) The ownership of the property cannot pass to Bevan and Christy because it was given to them by a will.
   (d) Bevan is a legal owner and Christy is an equitable owner.
   (e) Bevan is an equitable owner and Christy is a legal owner.

Answer: See Appendix C.

2. In the above scenario, Christy gives notice to Bevan in writing to state that she wants to sell her share in the property. She insists that she is entitled to half of the share of the property as it was left to two of them, so it makes sense that Abu gave each of them a half share. Which of the following are INCORRECT?
   (a) Christy is not entitled to half of the property in the absence of an express allocation in the will.
   (b) Christy and Bevan are joint tenants so they will have to convert the property by severance before selling.
   (c) Christy has not severed her share by giving written notice to Bevan that she wants to sell her share unless Bevan has accepted this.
   (d) Christy does not have to give a notice in writing to Bevan as she can just sell her share.
   (e) Bevan cannot go to court to stop the sale of the property if Christy so wishes.

Answer: See Appendix C.

6 The law of leases

Chapter overview

In addition to **freehold**, **leasehold** interest is the other **estate** included in the LPA 1925. As a result, leasehold interests are **proprietary** in nature. A **proprietary** right is guaranteed beyond the parties to the contract so a leaseholder's interest is protected not only against the landlord or **head-leaseholder** but against the whole world. This means that, if the landlord or head-leaseholder sold his/her property the new owner is bound by the interests held by a leaseholder (who is known as the **lessee**).

For instance, Jemina is a freeholder of a property for which she assigned a ten-year lease to Umar. After five years, Jemina sold the property to Michael while Umar was still in possession as a **lessee**. In this situation, Umar's leasehold interest is protected against Michael or anyone to whom Michael may sell or give. This is because Umar's leasehold right is **proprietary** which is protected against not only Jemina but also Michael or any other person to whom he transfers the property. The transfer may be a sale, gift, or another lease. Irrespective of the methods of transfer, Umar's interest is protected. In this way, **lease** is a very popular legal right which provides multiple enjoyment of the same piece of land at the same time.

So, a land can be held by a **freeholder**, a **leaseholder**, a **sub-leaseholder**, and so on at the same time. Although, a leaseholder's interest is protected as a **proprietary** right the scope of such protection depends on whether the **lease** is a **legal** or **equitable** one. **Legal leases** are those which have complied with the formalities for creation of a **legal lease**. On the other hand, **equitable leases** are those which have not complied with the formalities. However, although **legal leases** are more protected than **equitable** ones the latter are also protected by statutes such as the recognition of **overriding** status of equitable leases by the LRA 2002 in respect to **registered land** and the application of the **doctrine of notice** in respect to **unregistered land**.

DOI: 10.4324/9781003204954-6

6.1 Nature of a lease

A **lease** is a **proprietary** right which entitles a leaseholder certain statutory and **common law** rights against the **lessor** (landlord) under a **lease** such as **statutory** right to give notice to terminate a **lease**, right to stop the **lessor** from entering the leased property without the permission of the **lessee**. Most importantly, the **lessee** has a right to '**exclusive possession**' of the leased property which means that s/he has the exclusive right to exclude anyone including the landlord (**lessor**) from the property.

A **lease** can be short term or long term (which is known as a long **leasehold** or **term of years**). A short-term **lease** can be for a fixed term or period. A fixed-term **lease** is fixed for a certain time such as three months or one year. A periodic **tenancy** (or lease) renews once the fixed period or term expires. For example, after the expiry of the first six months fixed term or period a **lease** can become a periodic **tenancy** that would renew every month or week.

It is important for you to note that many people use the term '**lease**' and '**tenancy**' interchangeably. However, a '**lease**' is a preferable term for long-term leasehold property such as 20 years. On the other hand, '**tenancy**' is a preferable term for short-term lettings of residential properties.

6.2 Characteristics of a lease

A **lease** can be **legal** or **equitable** depending on how it was created. For instance, in order to be **legal** – a **lease** for more than three years must be made in a **deed**,[1] and a lease for more than seven years must be made in a **deed** as well as registered.[2] Also, a **lease** where the **leaseholder** is going to take possession in more than three months' time after its creation or assignment (also known as a **reversionary lease**) must also be registered.[3] Any **lease** which fails to comply with any of these requirements is **equitable**.

So, any **lease** that is for more than a period of three years but has not been made in a **deed**, or more than a period of seven years but neither has been made in a **deed** nor registered, or where the lease (for whatever term) is not going to be effected by possession until after a period of three months or longer and it was not registered, is equitable.[4] Based on this, the only **legal** lease that can be made orally and without registration is a **lease** for three years or less as long it

1 In writing together with one witness signing.
2 LP (MP) 1989, S. 1; LPA 1925, Ss. 52(1) (2) (d), 54 (d); LRA 2002, Ss. 4, 27 (2).
3 LRA 2002, S. 4 (1) (d).
4 LRA 2002, Ss. 7, 27 (1); and LPA 1925, S. 54 (2).

fulfils the statutory requirement such as (i) it starts at the date of creation not in future; and (ii) at best market rent obtainable.[5]

It is important for you to note that an **equitable lease** can be created by a **proprietary estoppel** where the lessor (assignor of the lease or landlord) made a representation that this was a **lease**, there was a reliance on that representation by the **lessee**, and based on the representation the **lessee** acted to his/her **detriment**.[6] Moreover, an **equitable lease** can be created by **constructive trusts** where the assignor of the **lease** assured the other party that no written contract was necessary.

The difference between a **legal** and **equitable** lease is that a legal lease is protected by entry into the **register**, so a purchaser is subject to the rights so protected. On the other hand, an **equitable lease** is not entered in the **register** so it would only be protected under the **doctrine of notice** (where the land is **unregistered**), and where the lease is protected as an **overriding interest** (**registered land**) such as **actual occupation**, a **lease** for the term of seven years or less, a legal **easement**.[7] Please note that a **licensee** (even in **actual occupation** of the property) cannot be protected as a holder of an **overriding interest** because a licensee's right is **personal** rather than equitable, unlike the lessee's right, which is **proprietary**.[8]

A lease can be created under the **statute** (statutory) or **common law**. The statutory definition of a **lease** is:

> 'Term of years absolute' means a term of years ... either certain or liable to determination by notice, re-entry, operation of law, or by a provision for cesser on redemption, or in any other event (other than the dropping of a life, or the determination of a determinable life interest); ... and in this definition the expression 'term of years' includes a term for less than a year, or for a year or years and a fraction of a year or from year to year.[9]

The above definition does not explicitly identify all the essential characteristics of a **lease** but one, i.e., a fixed term or a periodic term. However, there are two other essential characteristics of a **lease** such as the right of **exclusive possession** of a piece of land, and at a **rent**.[10] As a result, a **lease** has three essential characteristics, namely exclusive possession, a certain term, and a rent.

5 LRA 2002, Sch. 1 and 3.
6 For a discussion about proprietary estoppel, see Chapter 7.
7 LRA 2002, Sch. 1 and 3.
8 *Strand Securities v Caswell* [1965] Ch. 958.
9 LPA 1925, S. 205 (1) (XXVii).
10 *Street v Mountford* (1985) AC 809.

6.2.1 Exclusive possession

A **lease** creates a **proprietary** right which, as opposed to a **personal** right, creates an exclusive **possessory right**. Therefore, a **lessee** could assign his or her interest in land and such assignment is binding on any subsequent transferee of the head **lease** or even **freehold**.

> For instance, a **lessee** can assign a two-year sub-lease out of his/her three years lease, and this would be binding on the **freeholder** or head-lessor who assigned the three years **lease** or any purchaser of the property from them. Therefore, a **lessee**'s/**tenant**'s interest is **proprietary** and hence s/he can sue anyone (including the landowner) for **trespass**. S/he could also sue for **nuisance**. On the other hand, a **licensee** could do neither of these because his/her right is merely **personal**.

It is important for you to note that a right of **exclusive possession** of a **tenant** of the property can be created in a **lease** which is not similar to **exclusive occupation** which can be created in a **licence**. Unlike a right to **exclusive possession** in a **tenancy**, a right to **exclusive occupation** can be created in a **licence**. This is merely a **personal** right and enforceable between the parties who created this. For instance, a lodger may have **exclusive occupation** of the house or the room where s/he lives. In this situation, the lodger is a **licensee** who may not stop the **licensor** (the person who granted the license) from entering the house or room without permission. This also applies against a third party who bought the property from the **licensor**. Also, a **lessee** is protected by the statutory regime of the Rent Act 1977 (that sets up the **rent**), and the Housing Act 1988 (restricts the ability of landlords to remove **tenants**). For instance, a landlord usually needs to give only two months' notice to recover possession of a **lease**, whereas for a **licensee** four weeks' notice is required.[11]

Exclusive possession is the key element that distinguishes a **lease** from a **licence**. Due to the **personal** nature of a licensee's right and due to the **statutory protection** and **rent control**, landowners are often tempted to draw up agreements with potential occupiers of the land which merely create **licences**, not **leases**.[12] In most cases, this was attempted by seeking to deny the grant of '**exclusive possession**'. So, attaching labels to agreements – **tenancy** or **licence** – is not decisive. An agreement written under the title '**tenancy**' may be held a **licence** and **vice versa**. Therefore, the key test for '**exclusive possession**' is NOT based on the parties' intention BUT the substance of the rights they have created by agreement which can be identified from:

11 Housing Act 1998, S. 21; Protection from Eviction Act 1977, Ss. 3–5.
12 *Antoniades v Villiers* (1990) 1 AC 417.

- The surrounding circumstances of each case.
- The course of any negotiations prior to the grant of occupation.
- The nature of the property.
- The actual mode of occupation.[13]

It is important for you to note that there are exceptions where '**exclusive possession**' itself does not guarantee a lease i.e., exclusive possession is created by some ***bona fide*** (in good faith) relationship between the parties. For instance:

- Where a **mortgagee** (bank) is going into possession of the property and the **mortgagor/lessee** is still in possession. Here the lessee's **exclusive possession** is created out of a ***bona fide*** relationship between him/her and the bank. This is because, the **lessee** failed to keep up **mortgage** repayments, so their **exclusive possession** of the property is out of a good faith relationship with the bank.
- The occupation of a purchaser under an enforceable contract of sale. For instance, where the **lessee** entered into a contract to purchase the property and occupying the property on the basis of the contract to take effect after the end of the lease.
- Where the occupation is based on charity where the lessor allowed the occupier to possess the property as an act of kindness/charity.
- Where the occupation is based on friendship.
- Where the possessor is a service occupier, e.g., a hotel manager occupying a hotel room.[14]

It is very important for you to note that the right to '**exclusive possession**' must emanate or come from a person who himself/herself has the right. For instance, a right to '**exclusive possession**' must come from a **freeholder** or a **head-leaseholder** from whom the **lease** has been taken. So, a **licensee** cannot create a **lease** because they themselves do not have a right to **exclusive possession**. However, in exceptional circumstances the court may find a **tenancy** or **lease** where the lessor themselves did not have the right to **exclusive possession**. For instance, where a housing association assigns a tenancy to a council **tenant,** but they (the association) do not have '**exclusive possession**' themselves due to the council being the **freeholder** or **head-leaseholder** of the property. The court recognises this type of **lease** (non-proprietary lease) because otherwise the council **tenant** would not be able to hold the housing association responsible for breach of the terms of the **tenancy**.[15]

6.2.2 A term certain

A **lease** must be granted for a defined and certain period. The maximum duration of a **lease** must be definable at the beginning of a **lease** or **tenancy**. However, such a **lease** is terminable by a **break clause** before the end of the maximum duration.

13 *Street v Mountford* (1985) AC 809.
14 Per Lord Templeman in *Street v Mountford* (1985) AC 809.
15 *Bruton v London & Quadrant Housing Trust* (1999) UKHL 26.

For instance, the grant of a **lease** for ten years can include a **break clause** which gives either party an option to terminate the **tenancy** by giving six months' notice once the period of seven years is completed under the **lease**.

It is important for you to note that a lease created for an uncertain period of time is void. For instance, a **lease** for the duration of the COVID-19 pandemic is void for being of uncertain maximum duration. However, a lease for an uncertain period of time can be saved under the **common law** rule and/or **statute**.[16]

For instance, an agreement that assigned the occupier a lease of a piece of land until it was required for road widening can be a **lease** under an old **common law** rule which provided that "if the uncertain term was granted to an individual (but not to a company) then the agreement could be treated as a '**lease for life**'." A '**lease for life**' granted at a rent or for a payment is converted to a **lease** for 90 years terminable by death of the **tenant** (if earlier). However, in this situation the court must be satisfied that the parties originally intended a **lease for life**. Therefore, an uncertain lease cannot be saved in the absence of a valid consent or intention of the parties.

It is very important for you to note that in certain circumstances a **periodic tenancy** may be implied by the court in the absence of a term certain. For instance, a **periodic tenancy** is implied where a **tenant** has occupied the premises and paid a regular sum in rent to the landlord. In this way, a **tenancy** would continue in each successive term for a period in respect to which a payment of rent is paid or agreed to be paid. Thus, a monthly periodic **tenant** who has been in occupation for, say ten years has had 120 separate monthly tenancies.

In addition, there are certain restrictions imposed by law in terms of the maximum length of a **lease** for which it can be renewed, and the maximum period for which a **reversionary lease** (a **lease** that takes effect on a future date after its creation) can be created or assigned. Such as:

- **Perpetually renewable lease**: A lease that is renewable without restriction as to how many times that could be renewed is converted into a lease for 2000 years.[17]

16 *Berrisford v Mexfield* (2011) UKSC 52.
17 LPA 1925, Sch. 15 and S. 145.

- **Lease intended to start in more than 21 years**: A lease to start in more than 21 years after the instrument that creates it is void.[18]

6.2.3 Rent

A rent is generally payable in a **tenancy**. However, this is not a strict requirement as the LPA 1925 provided that 'a **term of years** ... *whether or not at a rent*'.[19] However, the payment of a rent strengthens the argument in favour of a **tenancy**. Therefore, **statutes** such as the Rent Acts and Housing Acts require a payment of rent. A rent can be paid in different ways:

- **A premium or fine**: This is a capital sum payable at the start of the **lease**.
- **A ground rent**: This is normally payable annually. However, it is important for you to note that a new legislation has been passed by the parliament which rendered payment of ground rent illegal.[20]
- **Service charge**: Paid monthly or annually to meet the cost of running and maintaining any common parts of the building.

Payment of rent can be implied. However, a non-payment of rent will always raise the question of whether this is a **tenancy** or **licence**. But remember that, a rent does not have to be paid in a monetary form. It is payable by goods, services or in kind. However, a rent must be a certain amount NOT an ever-changing sum.

6.3 Termination of a lease

A **lease** can be terminated in various ways. The most common ones are by lapse or effluxion of time, and by notice. For instance, a **lease** for five years can be terminated at the end of the term unless renewed. Similarly, a periodic **tenancy** (renewed every month) can be terminated by giving a month's notice by either party.

A **lease** can also be terminated by surrender where the **lessee** or **tenant** can surrender the **lease** before completion of the fixed term. However, the surrender must be accepted by the **lessor,** or the **lessee** must surrender according to the lease agreement. For instance, the lease agreement may provide that the **lessee** must surrender the lease if they become bankrupt or subject to administration.

Forfeiture is also a very common ground for termination of a **lease**. Although this is mostly invoked by landlords where a **tenant** or **lessee** fails to comply with a fundamental condition of the **lease** such as keeping up the payments of rent, a **tenant** can also invoke this method of termination where a landlord fails to keep up the repairs agreed under the lease agreement. A **forfeiture** of a **lease** is within the jurisdiction of

18 LPA 1925, S. 149 (3).
19 LPA 1925, S. 205(1)(xxvii).
20 Leasehold Reform (Ground Rent) Act 2021.

the Lands Tribunal which is also known as the First Tier Tribunal (Property Chamber). Where a party to a **lease** cannot invoke **forfeiture,** they can still terminate it by showing a **repudiatory breach of contract**. This is a valuable remedy available particularly for the **tenants** against landlords where '**forfeiture**' is not available. For instance, where the landlord continuously failed or refused to carry out repairs of the property under the terms of the **tenancy**.

Another popular way to terminate a **lease** is by merging the **leasehold** interest with a new one. For instance, if A was a leaseholder of a ground floor shop for 99 years and now, he has been assigned a 199-year **lease** of the whole building then A's leasehold interest in the ground floor shop is terminated by merger of that interest with the new **lease** of the entire building.

A lease can also be terminated by enlargement. This is a statutory arrangement where long leases can be enlarged to freehold. For instance, in the above example, A can buy the freehold of the whole building where his/her lease of the ground floor shop will be enlarged. Also, another way of enlargement can occur where a **lease** of 300 years with 200 years left to run can be enlarged to a **freehold** as a **legal** right.[21]

It is very important for you to note that in a very rare situation, a **lease** can be terminated by a **disclaimer** from the **tenant**. For instance, when a **tenant** denies the superior title of the landlord. This happens when a **tenant** has been asked to pay a rent to two different landlords and the former denied one of the latter's **freehold** or head-lease interest in the piece of land.

A **lease** can also be terminated by **frustration**. This is a common incident where there are fundamental changes of circumstances after commencement of the **lease**. For instance, if the **lessee** started to run business from his/her property which was included as a cause for frustration of the **lease** in the lease agreement.

6.4 Leasehold covenants

Leasehold **covenants** are conditions attached to the **lease** or **tenancy** which are binding on the parties i.e., landlord and **tenant**. For instance, a condition stating that you cannot keep a pet in the property without obtaining written permission from the landlord. Both landlord and **tenant** can be subject to **covenants**. The person who promised or assumed a duty is known as a '**covenantor**'; and the person to whom a promise is made, or duty assumed is known as a '**covenantee**'. A **covenant** can involve various promises. For instance, **covenants** to pay rent, council taxes, take home and content insurance, conduct repairing work.[22]

21 LPA 1925, S. 153.
22 Landlord and Tenant Act 1927, s. 19(1) (a).

It is important for you to note that **covenants** can be made expressly or impliedly. Whereas an expressly promised **covenant** must be written down in a clause in the **tenancy** agreement, a covenant can be implied by law. For instance, the Homes (Fitness for Human Habitation) Act 2018 implicated some duties on the landlord such as ensuring that the property is safe and suitable for human habitation. These duties include carrying out of repairs to address issues with heating, damp, mould, access to natural light, sanitation, drainage, fire safety, electrical hazards and so on.

Chapter revision points

- A **lease** is a **proprietary** right in a piece of land as opposed to a **personal** one. A lease is also known as **term of years**, **tenancy**, sub-lease, and leasehold estate. The three key essential elements of a lease are – **exclusive possession**, a certain term, and payment of rent.
- A lease can be **legal** and **equitable**.
- **Legal** leases are:
  - Leases for three years or less – no formalities required.
  - Leases for more than three years BUT less than seven years – a deed is necessary.
  - Leases for more than seven years – need registration.
  - Leases where possession is postponed for more than three months after the lease is granted – need registration.
- **Equitable** leases are:
  - Leases for more than three years BUT less than seven years – if no deed is executed.
  - Leases for more than seven years assigned out of registered land – if not registered.
  - Leases where possession is postponed for more than three months after the lease is granted – if not registered.
  - **Proprietary estoppel** leases.
  - **Constructive trusts** (where the assignor of a lease assured the other party that no written contract is necessary).
- A **lease** can be terminated in the following ways:
  - By effluxion of time.
  - By forfeiture.
  - By notice (including 'break clause').
  - By merger.
  - By surrender.
  - By enlargement.
  - By disclaimer.

- By frustration.
- By repudiatory breach of contract.

- Both landlord and **tenant** can be subject to conditions which are expressly promised or impliedly imposed on them. Express promises are written down in clauses of the **tenancy** agreement. However, implied duties are imposed by statutes such as Homes (Fitness for Human Habitation) Act 2018.

Multiple choice question

Jemina granted Umar a lease (in a deed) of her studio flat for five years at a market rent. The agreement is titled 'licence agreement'. Which one of the following is CORRECT?

(a) The lease is an equitable lease because it has not been registered.
(b) The agreement is not a lease because it does not state if exclusive possession has been granted.
(c) The agreement is not a lease because the rent has not been specifically set out.
(d) The agreement is a licence because its title is 'licence agreement'.
(e) The agreement is a lease because the term is certain for five years, exclusive possession can be implied, and market rent has been specified – all meet the legal requirement.

Answer: See Appendix C.

7 Licences and proprietary estoppel

Chapter Overview

In Chapter 1, the differences between a **personal** and **proprietary** right were discussed. It is very important for you to remember that the key difference between these two types of rights is that a **personal** right is not binding on a third party, but a **proprietary** right is. As a result, a **personal right** (such as **licence**) is not binding on a purchaser (a third party) who purchased the property (in respect to which a **licence** is held) from the **licensor**. Conversely, a **proprietary right** (such as **estoppel**) is binding on a purchaser. This chapter addresses this difference in respect to **licences** and **proprietary estoppel**.

Licences are personal rights to enjoy some rights or privileges over someone else's land.

For instance, Jemina (the **registered proprietor** of a house) allowed her friend, Avery, to live in the spare bedroom until the latter could find another accommodation. This is a **personal right** which Avery can only enforce against Jemina. She cannot enforce this right against Umar, a third party, who purchased the house from Jemina. However, Jemina can revoke the **licence** given to Avery at any time by giving a reasonable notice because of the personal nature of the **licence**.

On the contrary, a **proprietary estoppel** (PE) is **proprietary** in nature so it can bind a third party.

For instance, if Jemina asked Avery to quit her job so she could look after Jemina and her house; and Jemina promised that Avery will always have a right to stay in the house and based on this promise Avery quit her job to live in the house and looked after Jemina – this can create a PE in Avery's favour. As a result, if Jemina and Avery fell out and the former decided to sell the house to Umar, then Avery can make a claim under PE against Jemina and Umar would be bound by this claim

DOI: 10.4324/9781003204954-7

if upheld by the court because this is a **proprietary right**. Although both **licences** and PE are informally created the latter can lead to ownership or title to the land, whereas the former can only create a **personal right**. However, it is important for you to note that there are specific legal requirements to create a PE (see below).

7.1 The nature and effect of a licence

A **licence** is a permission given by the owner of a piece of land to another person, who may or may not own the land or part of it themselves, to use the owner's land for some specific purposes. For instance, you can give permission to an ice cream seller to park his/her van in your land to sell ice cream. This is an example of an expressly created **licence**. However, a **licence** can be created impliedly as well such as you have impliedly given permission to the postman to enter your land (front garden/porch) to deliver the posts through your front door. As discussed above, the nature of a **licence** is merely personal so the **licensor** (who gave the permission) can revoke the **licence** by giving a very short notice. Many students ask this question – if a **licence** can be revoked at any time why it is necessary in the first place? The answer to this question is that, without a **licence** a **licensee** (to whom a permission is given) would be a **trespasser**, which is illegal. To clarify this situation, I want to give an example.

Think about going to a cinema. When you buy a ticket to watch a movie your legal status is a **licensee**. You have a right to enter the cinema and watch the movie you have paid for – which is a personal right. You will have to leave the cinema within a reasonable time after the movie ends. You cannot live in the cinema overnight as your **licence** is limited to just watching the movie. Also, the **licensor** (the cinema management) can legally revoke the **licence** at any time if you do not comply with the terms of the **licence**, such as if you cause an obstruction to other customers in the cinema.

Please note that the nature and effect of a **licence** depend on the type of **licence** given. The following section discussed this.

7.2 Types of licence

Licences are classified according to the functions they serve, the circumstances in which they arise, or the way in which they are created. If a **licence** is created to allow or permit an entry to a building for a very short time, there is no formality required to create the **licence** or revoke the same.

For instance, if you allow your neighbour to park their car on your land on Christmas evening this year – this is a **bare licence** which would be automatically revoked the next morning, and you would not need to follow any formalities to revoke this.

On the other hand, in a contractual **licence** (like the example of buying a cinema ticket – see the above section), the **licensor** would need to follow the terms agreed to revoke the licence.

For instance, in the cinema ticket situation the **licensor** will have to give your money back if they want to cancel the showing of the movie due to unforeseen circumstances beyond their control. Also, you may be able to claim some compensation, but you do not have the right to compel the cinema management to play the movie in the scheduled time – because your right is a **personal** right not **proprietary**, and the **licence** given to you has been revoked by the **licensor**.

- **Bare licences**: These licences are the most common form where a **licensor** gives permission to a **licensee** to enter upon his/her land and carry out some activities there. The permission is given voluntarily by the owner who received no money or remuneration in return. For example, express permission given to an engineer to come and repair your TV and broadband; implied permission to a postman to come and deliver a parcel. The **licensor** may terminate or revoke the **licence** by giving a reasonable notice to the **licensee**, and the **licensee** has no claim in **damages** or **specific performance** should this happen. Hence, if you called an engineer, within a reasonable time before the scheduled appointment, i.e., three days, to cancel a scheduled visit they do not have any claim for **damages** or **specific performance**.
- **Licences coupled with an interest or grant**: Sometimes a permission can be given to the **licensee** because it is needed to exercise another interest in a piece of land already granted. For example, a ***profit a prendre***[1] coupled with a licence can be given to enter the land and remain there for an appropriate time. The **licence** will last for as long as the profit exists and will be enforceable against whomsoever the profit is enforceable against because it is an inherent component of the greater right. For instance, a farmer sold their pumpkins to a supermarket who were allowed to enter the farmland and pick the pumpkins. The agreement to sell the pumpkins included a **licence** to stay in the farmland

1 *Profits á prendre* – see Chapter 8.

for a period of time when the supermarket's employee/representative would reasonably need to pick the pumpkins.

- **Contractual licences**: Contractual licences are similar to **bare licences** with the important difference being that those are granted to the **licensee** in return for **consideration**. For example, purchasing a cinema ticket or a parking permit, and occupying a hotel room.

7.3 Proprietary estoppel (PE)

In order to create or transfer a **proprietary right** in a piece of land the law requires that such a right must be completed in writing.[2] As a result, the formal requirement to create an interest in land in writing applies to most transfers of land such as a **will**, **deed** or registered **dispositions**, leases over three years to run. However, PE is an exception to the formality requirements for creating interests in a piece of land.[3] This is because the right or privilege conferred by a PE will arise out of the conduct of the parties, usually because of some assurance made by the landowner, which is relied upon by the person claiming the right.

For instance, your father asked you to quit your job so you could come to live with him in his house and become his carer; he also told you that you would not need to worry about your future as he would ensure this for you; and based on these representations you quit your job and became his carer. However, after his death you found out that in a **will**, he left all his property to a charity but nothing for you – this is a case of PE. Although this was created informally without writing, you may be entitled to claim a right in the property or other remedy such as a cash sum proportionate to the **detriment** that you have suffered.

It is important for you to know that a valid claim of PE can also be a ground for defence against allegation of **trespass** or **nuisance** by the landowner.

To claim a PE the following five conditions (also known as the five probanda) must be fulfilled:

- The claimant must have made a mistake as to their legal rights over some land belonging to another (landowner).
- The true landowner must know of the claimant's mistaken belief.
- The claimant must have spent money or carried out some activities under the faith of that mistaken belief.

2 Law of Property (Miscellaneous Provisions) Act 1989, S. 2.
3 LPA 1925, S. 53(2); and S. 2(5) LP (MP) Act 1989, S. 2(5).

- The landowner must have encouraged the claimant to spend money, either directly, or by abstaining from enforcing their legal rights.
- The owner of the piece of land over which the right is claimed must know of the existence of their own rights, and that these are inconsistent with the alleged rights of the claimant.[4]

The above conditions were developed to adopt a more flexible approach to **proprietary estoppel**. However, a claimant will be able to establish an **estoppel** if they can prove the four criteria, namely an **assurance**, **reliance**, a **detriment**, and circumstances in which it would be **unconscionable** to deny a remedy to the claimant.[5] It is important for you to note that the landowner's knowledge of the claimant's belief (albeit mistaken) is not always necessary as long as the claimant can establish that the landowner's encouragement was entirely consistent with the PE to exist.[6] Also, the court is inclined to take into account the claimant's belief more seriously in comparison to the knowledge of the landowner.[7]

Please note that PE cannot be invoked by the back door to circumvent the requirement of a written document to create or transfer a proprietary right. In other words, the court is not going to enforce an oral agreement under the auspices of PE.[8]

7.3.1 The assurance

The landowner must have given some kind of assurance to the claimant that either (i) the landowner would refrain from exercising his/her strict legal rights over his/her own land; or (ii) the claimant might have some present or future rights over that land. Although an assurance must be clear, it is not necessary that such assurance would concern any specific property right on the land such as ownership, a **lease**. It is enough if there are some general assurances particularly in the context of a family arrangement. Therefore, if the claimant and defendant are family members (e.g., father/mother vs son/daughter) then some general assurances would suffice, i.e., an assurance that the claimant will always have a roof over him/her.[9] However, in the context of a commercial arrangement (e.g., between business partners) more specific assurance would be necessary.[10]

The landowner can assure the claimant by (i) acquiescence, i.e., standing by while the claimant acts detrimentally; or (ii) silent inaction, i.e., encourage to continue.

4 *Wilmott v Barber* (1880) 15 ChD 96.
5 *Taylor Fashions v Liverpool Victoria Trustees* (1982) QB 133.
6 *Hoyl Group Ltd v Cromer Town Council* (2015) EWCA Civ 782.
7 *Thorner v Major* (2009) 1 WLR 776.
8 *Cobbe v Yeoman's Row Management* [2008] UKHL 55.
9 *Thorner v Major* (2009) 1 WLR 776.
10 *Cobbe v Yeoman's Row Management* [2008] UKHL 55.

Circumvention of formality (the requirement of a written document) is not permissible BUT remedying of **unconscionability** is desirable, and it is perfectly possible for a PE to exist independently of a failed or missing contract. However, the court must approach a claim of estoppel with scepticism when the only evidence of an assurance is the uncorroborated evidence of the claimant.[11]

7.3.2 The reliance

The claimant must rely on the assurance, in that it must be possible to show that s/he intended to behave differently because the assurance had been made. However, it is sufficient if the claimant reasonably relies on the assurance, even if the landowner did not intend that s/he should so rely.[12] It is important for you to note that in this situation the court will need to see a sufficient link between the assurance made and the detriment incurred by the claimant. If clear assurance has been made and detriment has been suffered, it is permissible for the court to assume that reliance has occurred.[13] The crucial point seems to be that there will be no reliance only when it can be shown that the claimant would have incurred the detriment irrespective of the defendant's conduct.[14]

7.3.3 The detriment

PE cannot be established unless the claimant can prove that s/he has suffered some detriment in reliance on the assurance. However, the detriment must be incurred by the person to whom the assurance was made.[15] It may take any of the following forms, such as the claimant has:

- Spent money on the land or advanced money to the landowner in reliance on the assurance.
- Physically improved the land in some way.
- Has devoted time and care to the needs of the landowner.

It is important for you to note that it is not necessary that the detriment be related to land at all. For instance, it would suffice if the claimant has spent money in other ways on the faith of an assurance or s/he has derived some benefits for his/her association with the landowner, but such association does not outweigh their detrimental reliance.

Jemina can make a claim under PE if she had lived in her father's house for ten years and spent money in buying medicines for the latter. This is because the

11 *Creasy v Sole* [2013] EWHC 1410.
12 *Thorner v Major* (2009) 1 WLR 776.
13 *Greasley v Cooke* [1980] 3 All ER 710.
14 *Orgee v Orgee* [1997] EGCS 152.
15 *Lloyd v Dugdale* [2001] EWCA Civ 1754.

benefit of living with her father does not outweigh the detriment which she suffered by leaving her job to look after her elderly father. Also, spending to buy her father's medicines also counts as a detriment although this is not a spending related to her father's house.

7.3.4 The unconscionability

'Unconscionability' is at the very essence of a PE claim. It means unfairness. It is normally the promisor's knowledge of the detriment that is being suffered by the promisee in reliance on the former's promise which makes it 'unconscionable' for him/her to step back from it."[16] Unconscionability may exist even when the assurance is withdrawn after detrimental reliance.[17]

For instance, if the promisor has withdrawn his/her promises after the claimant or promisee has acted to his/her detriment. The promisor may have done this fraudulently or because the relationship between the promisor and promisee broke down.

It is very important for you to remember that a claimant does not have to prove fraud by the defendant although there are elements of fraud in the concept.[18]

7.4 Successful pleas of proprietary estoppel

Both claimant and defendant can make a valid plea of **proprietary estoppel**. A claim of PE operates as a sword (as a claim in itself). For instance, when a claimant makes a valid claim to exclude the landowner from denying the right claimed. But it operates as a shield (as a defence) when a defendant makes a valid defence against a claim by a landlord for a violation of **restrictive covenant**, **nuisance**, and **trespass**.

It is important for you to note that the remedy for a valid PE claim is retrospective, i.e., effective from the date of the claim, but not prospective, i.e., from the date of judgement of the court. For instance, a remedy can be either of the following:

- Expectation-based, i.e., the claimant gets that which was promised.
- Reliance-based, i.e., the claimant gets that which is commensurate with the extent of their detrimental reliance.

16 *Gillett v Holt* [2001] Ch 210.
17 Ibid.
18 *Orgee v Orgee* [1997] EGCS 152.

- A mixture of the two PROVIDED THAT the **unconscionability** has been taken into account.

However, it is important for you to note that the remedy must be proportionate to the expectation, reliance, and actual conduct of the parties and detriment.

7.5 The effect of proprietary estoppel on third parties

This is a very common scenario where the promisor (landowner) has sold the property in respect to which a PE claim was made or about to be made. As stated above, a PE is a **proprietary right** which is binding on third parties. As a result, a valid and successful PE claim is binding on a purchaser who purchased the property from the promisor.

For instance, if Jemina (the promisor) sold a property to Umar (a third party) because she fell out with the claimant (Avery), a PE claim by Avery can be made against Jemina, and Umar would be bound by that claim if upheld by the court.

Please note that a PE claim can be made even where the landowner became bankrupt, and the property fell in the hands of the **trustee in bankruptcy** or administrator. In this situation, a claimant's right will be protected with retrospective effect, i.e., their right at the date of occurrence of the incident that led to a PE claim. This is the **statutory** position for registered title land.[19]

7.6 The intersection between proprietary estoppel and constructive trusts

A question often arises – should a claim be made under PE or constructive trust (CT)? Although it is quite common to make a claim both under PE and CT, the court often considers either of these because the result or outcome might be the same.[20] However, PE and CT are similar but not the same: see Table 7.1. This is because these two share some common features, but the **evidential burden** is higher in CT. For instance, claims under CT are available in extremely limited circumstances because the 'assurance' requirement in a CT needs to satisfy a higher evidential threshold, e.g., **common intention**. On the contrary, claims under PE are available in a wide range of circumstances because proof of a 'unilateral assurance' would suffice. More

19 LRA 2002, S. 116.
20 See *Aspden v Elvy* [2012] EWHC 1387 – discussed in Chapter 4.

Table 7.1 The comparative features between PE and CT

Grounds	PE	CT
Evidential burden	**Lower** – assurance by the promisor (unilateral assurance).	**Higher** – An express, or implied, or imputed **common intention**.
Nature of claim (outcome)	Where the claimant is looking for a ***property right*** or a ***cash lump sum***.	Where a claimant is looking for a ***fair share*** in ***co-ownership*** situation.
Nature of claim (commonality)	Disputes between strangers as well as between family members or friends.	Disputes between co-owners, i.e., matrimonial or quasi-matrimonial disputes concerning a family home.
Circumventing formal requirement	Cannot circumvent the formal requirement of writing.	Can circumvent the formal requirement of writing.
Application of statutes	Claim is based on **equity** and no **statutes** apply.	Statutes such as TOLATA 1996 would apply.

importantly, a claim under PE is very common where the claimant is looking for a property right or a cash lump sum from the defendant. On the other hand, a claim under CT is very common where the claimant is looking for a fair share in a property which the claimant as well as defendant own in law and/or equity (a **co-ownership** situation).[21] Additionally, whereas a CT claim is very commonly relied on in matrimonial or quasi-matrimonial disputes concerning a family home, a PE claim is very commonly made in disputes between strangers and family members or friends.

Please note that, in both PE and CT claims, the '**unconscionability**' criterion is particularly important to prove. However, the nature of **unconscionability** is not the same in these claims. On the one hand, in a PE claim the **unconscionability** lies on the denial of a promise which was unilaterally made by the **promisor** (defendant) and reasonably relied on by the claimant (albeit mistakenly) – so the difference between the promise and detrimental reliance shows a lack of agreement between the parties.[22] On the other hand, in a CT claim a **common intention** can be discerned from the conduct of the parties where they orally agreed on something – so there is no difference between what was promised and what was relied on to **detriment**. Moreover, it is sometimes difficult to prove **unconscionability** against the defendant (**promisor**) in

21 See Chapter 4 for further analysis of a CT situation.

22 Based on this lack of agreement – there are differences on the remedy such as expectation based *versus* reliance based.

order to enforce a verbal agreement in a CT claim because here the parties intended but failed to conclude a written contract. On the contrary, it is not so difficult to prove **unconscionability** against a **promisor** in a PE claim because here the defendant made the promise which led to the claimant's detrimental reliance. Therefore, in a CT claim a verbal agreement can be enforced but not in a PE claim (because in a PE claim the parties lack agreement). In this regard, the law of CT is developing to explain how some otherwise unenforceable contracts can be enforced.[23]

Whereas '**unconscionability**' is a deciding factor in a PE claim, the **statute** has excused a CT claim from the formality requirement to be made in writing.[24] Whereas a CT claim may be remedied by awarding ownership in a family home (TOLATA 1996 – trust of land) or enforcement of an oral agreement (in a **constructive trust** in the absence of a written document), the outcome of a PE claim can be more flexible, such as an award may include a **proprietary right**, **personal right**, or no right at all. However, please remember that both **proprietary estoppel** and **constructive trusts** are **proprietary** as well as **equitable** doctrines. There are also other common features of a PE and CT such as detriment caused by a party, reliance on an assurance, contribution to the detriment, and **unconscionability**. However, there are a few thin dividing lines between these two: see Figure 7.1 and the adjacent discussion.

Chapter revision points

- **Licences** are **personal** rights opposed to **proprietary rights** in land.
- Licences can be **bare**, coupled with an interest or grant, and contractual.
- Depending on the type of a **licence**, the **licensor** can revoke it at any time with or without giving a reasonable notice for revocation.
- A claim of PE must satisfy four key criteria – a representation by the landowner, a reliance by the claimant, a detriment suffered by the claimant, and **unconscionability** on behalf of the claimant.
- A successful claim of a **licence** and PE is a defence against a claim of **trespass** by the landowner.
- Although sometimes the outcome of a claim under PE and CT can be the same, the criteria to establish a claim are not same.
- Whereas a CT claim is more common in a **co-ownership** situation in a family home, a PE claim is more common in disputes between strangers as well as between family members or friends.
- The law is developing to enforce a verbal agreement between the parties in a CT situation.
- Both PE and CT are **proprietary** as well as **equitable** doctrines.

23 *Matchmove v Dowding* [2016] EWCA Civ 1233.
24 LPA 1925, S. 53 (2); and LP (MP) Act 1989, S. 2 (5).

Multiple choice question

In which of the following situations an interest under proprietary estoppel will arise?

(a) A claimant will be able to establish an estoppel if they can prove an assurance, reliance and detriment in circumstances in which it would be unconscionable to deny a remedy to the claimant.
(b) A claimant will be able to establish an estoppel only if the assurance or promise has been expressly communicated to them.
(c) A claimant will be able to establish an estoppel if the detriment occurred, irrespective of whether such occurrence was the result of the reliance or not.
(d) A claimant will be able to establish an estoppel where the promise is not directly made to him.
(e) A claimant will be able to establish an estoppel to enforce an oral agreement which the parties intended but failed to conclude in writing.

Answer: See Appendix C.

8 Easements and *profits à prendre*

Chapter overview

Easements are legal rights which a landowner enjoys over another neighbouring land. A common example of an easement is a 'right of way over your neighbour's land'. The purpose of an easement is to facilitate the beneficial enjoyment of a land. However, the beneficial enjoyment must not be too burdensome on the burdened land over which the easement exists. Also, the beneficial enjoyment includes those which would benefit the land only rather than the landowner. For instance, your right of way over your neighbour's land is for the benefit of your land but a right to pick apples from your neighbour's orchard is not an easement but a licence, which is a personal right. Therefore, an easement is a **proprietary** right which you can enforce against a third party. In the example given in Figure 8.1, House A enjoys an easement over House B which has given the former a right to use the latter's garden for sunbathing. This is an easement right which is **proprietary** in nature.

> Because **easements** are **proprietary** rights, the owner of House A can enforce his easement right to sunbathe against a new purchaser who just bought House B. Similarly, any person who would buy House A is going to enjoy the easement rights against House B. Therefore, the benefits and burdens of an easement can pass on to a new owner with the transfer of both the benefited and burdened land. Please note that a **benefited land** is known as '**the dominant tenement**' and a burdened land is known as 'the servient tenement'.

Please also note that the owner of a burdened land does not need to spend money to upkeep an easement. However, the owner of a **benefited land** has a positive obligation to contribute to the expenditures that are necessary to upkeep the easement.

DOI: 10.4324/9781003204954-8

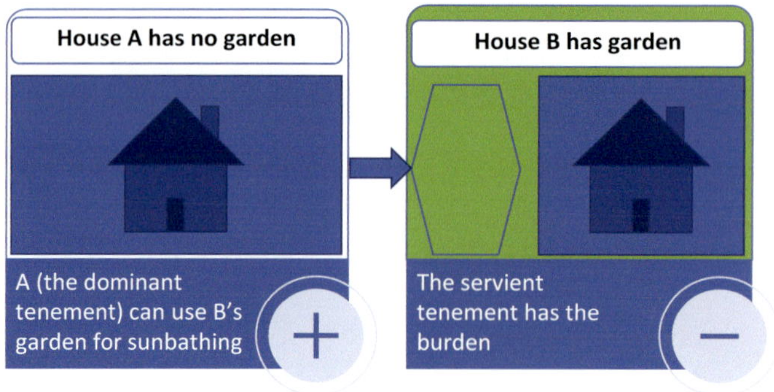

Figure 8.1 The right of easement in a neighbour's land.

8.1 Licences versus easements

Licences are very close to **easements**, and it is sometimes difficult to distinguish between these two. The following are instances where both licences and easements can be argued:

- Parking your car on your neighbour's land.
- Children playing football in an empty land belonging to another (neighbour).
- Using a neighbour's garden for a party.

In the above examples, the nature of the benefit that you can enjoy on a neighbour's land depends on whether the benefit is a **personal** or **proprietary** in nature. You may recall from the discussions in previous chapters (Chapters 1 and 7) that a **licence** is merely a **contractual or personal right** which is distinguishable from a **lease** and/or **easement** which is **proprietary**.

For instance, your neighbour may have allowed you to park your car on their land as an act of kindness which is merely a personal right (a **licence**), and so it can be revoked by your neighbour by giving you a short notice. On the other hand, if your right to park on your neighbour's land is due to the beneficial enjoyment of your own land because you do not have a parking space in your own land, this is a **proprietary right** – which is binding on not only your current neighbour who granted the easement but also any other person who would buy or inherit from them.

8.2 Characteristics of an easement

Not every right over your neighbour's land can be an **easement**. As discussed in the above section, a right to park on your neighbour's land can be a **licence** or a **lease** or an **easement**. Therefore, the nature of a right of **easement** would depend on a few key characteristics. Such as:

(a) **There must be a dominant and a servient tenement**: Unlike a profit, which may exist in gross (i.e., detached from the ownership of land), an **easement** cannot exist independently of the ownership of land. Therefore, you need to be an owner of a land to enjoy an **easement** right over your neighbour's land.

(b) **The easement must accommodate the dominant tenement**: The right granted must not simply confer a personal advantage unconnected with the land; it must increase the normal enjoyment of the land. For instance, use of the canal to keep a boat.[1]

(c) **The dominant and servient tenements must be owned or occupied by different persons**: A person cannot have an easement over his own land. For instance, you cannot claim a right of way over your own land. You actually do not need to make any such claim because as an owner you already have the right to reasonable enjoyment of your land. Note, however, the concept of a '**quasi-easement**', discussed below.[2]

(d) **The easement must be capable of forming the subject-matter of a grant**: An easement must originate in a **grant**, whether express, implied, or presumed, certain conditions must be fulfilled:

- There must be both a capable grantor and a capable grantee who are over 18 years old and persons of sound mind.
- The right must be sufficiently definite and clearly outlined.
- The right must be within the general nature of rights capable of existing as **easements** (such as a right of way and a right to light NOT right to have a view).[3]

It is very important for you to remember that like other **proprietary** rights **easements** can be **legal** or **equitable**. It is very important for the purchaser of a piece of land to discover whether a third party has an **easement** right that is enforceable against the land and, if so, what is the nature and extent of such a right, i.e., **legal** or **equitable**. The distinction between **legal** and **equitable easements** is important because different methods of creation apply to each category. The distinction is also crucial in determining whether an **easement** runs with the land, i.e., passes to a new owner on transfer of either the **dominant tenement** or **servient tenement**, to be enforceable by or against the new owner. These points are discussed below.

8.2.1 Legal easements

For an **easement** to be legal the following criteria must be fulfilled:

1. It must comply with the definitions of a legal estate, i.e., it is equivalent to either a ***fee simple*** or a ***term of years***.[4] This means a legal right of way can only be granted or created with respect to a **freehold** or **leasehold** land. Also, the right of way must be held for a period for which a **freehold** or **leasehold** interest can be created in law. This means an **easement** must be held for the duration of

1 *Hill v Tupper* (1863) 2 H & C 121.
2 For quasi-easement, see Section 8.3.
3 *Re Ellenborough Park* (1956) Ch 131.
4 LPA 1925, S. 1(2)(a).

holding the **freehold** or **leasehold** and must not extinguish by express or implied release or termination or abandonment, or where the purpose of the **easement** has ceased such as the **benefited land** now has its own parking.

2. It must comply with **conveyancing** and registration requirements, e.g., **deed**, **registration**, **prescription**. In other words, it must be created in writing unless exempted by law. For instance, a legal easement created by a **grant** from the landowner of the **burdened land** must be in writing. However, a **legal** easement by long use (**prescription**) or **proprietary estoppel** does not need to be in writing.

8.2.2 Equitable easements

In contrast to the criteria discussed in Section 8.2.1 for creating a **legal easement**, an easement can be **equitable** because it failed to comply with the **legal** requirements for creating a **legal easement**. For instance, an equitable easement that failed to comply with the conveyancing and registration requirements, e.g., not created by **deed** (an enforceable written document), or not registered in the land registry. This includes an **easement** held for a period other than either a **fee simple** or a **term of years**. For instance, a temporary **easement** granted for a certain time at the end of which the **benefited land** would no longer benefit from it, such as where the **benefited land** would have its own parking that can be accessible from the public road as a result of a new extension of the road.

You may remember from the discussions in Chapters 2 and 3 that different laws apply to **equitable** interests in **registered** and **unregistered** land. As a result, in order to protect an **equitable easement**, it is very important that it is protected according to the applicable laws. For instance:

Unregistered land:

- An **equitable easement** is registrable as Class D (iii) **land charges** under the LCA 1972, if the land is **unregistered**.
- An **equitable easement** must be registered to bind a subsequent purchaser of the **servient tenement**. If not registered it is void against a purchaser of the land but not against someone who received the land as a gift or by succession.

  There is an exception to the above rules, which is that an **equitable easement** created by **proprietary estoppel** does not need **registration**. Instead, the **doctrine of notice** would apply.

Registered land:

- An **equitable easement** can be registered in the **charges register**. Please note that this is not mandatory but the **land registry** encourages registration so the register can look like more of a mirror image.[5]

5 For 'mirror image', please see Chapter 3.

8.3 Creation of easements

An **easement** may be created either by a **reservation** or a **grant**. See Figure 8.2. Both **reservation** and **grant** can be express or implied.

An **easement** is created by express reservation where the owner of a **dominant tenement** deliberately and expressly keeps an **easement** right for himself when he sells or leases part of his land to another person. A reservation operates by way of re-grant, (i.e., the purchaser is deemed to have granted the easement to the seller). Therefore, if there is any ambiguity in the definition of the easement which cannot be dispelled by a consideration of the surrounding circumstances, the grant will be construed against the grantor, (i.e. in this case the purchaser). A reservation can be implied where the **easement** was necessary or intended. For instance, an **easement** of necessity can be implied where the owner of the **dominant tenement** reserves his/her right of way across the **servient tenement** by conduct. Such as, where there is no other way to access the **dominant tenement** from the main road except that over the **servient tenement** and the owner of the **dominant tenement** has not expressly reserved his right of way over the latter. This is an **easement** by necessity. However, an **easemen**t can be impliedly created if the reservation was intended by the parties such as where the owners of the **dominant** and **servient** tenements intended that the former could park his/her car in the latter's car park but nothing was mentioned in a **deed** about this.

It is important for you to understand that an express **grant** is self-explanatory. The owner of the **servient tenement** deliberately grants the right over his/her land to the owner of the **dominant tenement**.

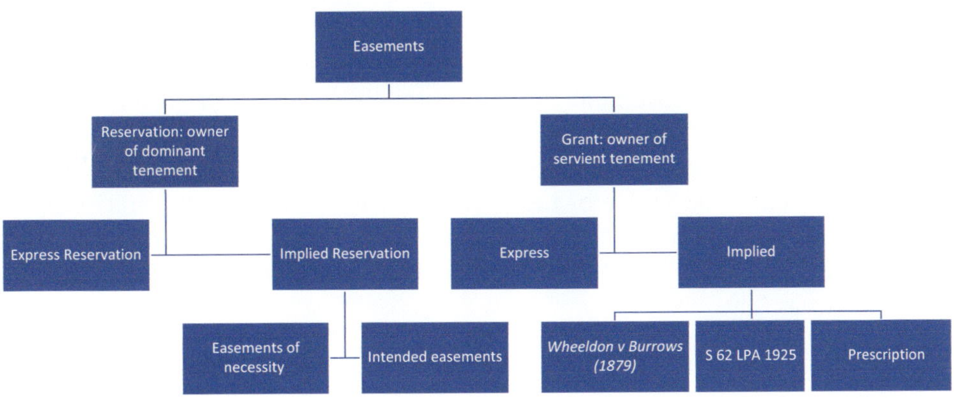

Figure 8.2 Methods of creating easements.

For instance, Jemina sold part of her land to Umar. Umar, the owner of the **servient tenement**, granted Jemina a right of way over his land. However, you must know that this can be done impliedly as well. For instance, in this situation between Jemina and Umar, the latter (Umar) granted a right of way over his land to the former (Jemina) without executing any deed to that effect but Umar impliedly granted this right of way to Jemina because she enjoyed the same right of way while she was the owner of that part of the land which is now owned by Umar.

Common law recognises **easement**-like rights (also known as a **quasi-easement**) if the following THREE conditions are met:

1. The easement must be continuous and apparent.
2. The easement must be necessary to the reasonable enjoyment of the property granted.
3. The easement must have been used by the common owner at the time of the grant for the benefit of the part granted.[6]

The **statute** also recognises an implied grant in a similar situation as under the **common law**. However, the statutory provision only applies where the land is sold by **deed** or **registration**, and for this reason it can only create a **legal easement**. Under the **statute**, in addition to the circumstances under the common law (outlined above), the following must be present:

- There must be a **conveyance**. This does not, for example, include an agreement for a **lease**, and in such a case the **common law** rule may still be relevant.
- There must be a **diversity of occupation** of the two tenements (pieces of land) at the time of the **conveyance**.
- The right or privilege should 'appertain or be reputed to appertain' to the land (i.e., be attached to the land or believed to do so) or enjoyed with the land at the time of the **conveyance**. Please note that, if the privilege has already been revoked, no **easement** can arise through the operation of the statutory provision.
- The statutory provision cannot convert into **easements** those rights which are in their nature incapable of being **easements**, such as the intermittent consensual privilege enjoyed by the claimant.[7] This can happen when you were allowed to use your neighbour's car park occasionally, i.e., on Easter Sunday, Christmas Day.

6 *Wheeldon v Burrows* [1879] 12 (Ch) D 31.
7 LPA 1925, S. 62.

Therefore, both **common law** and **statute** recognised already-existing **easements** between a **dominant** and **servient** tenement.

For instance, Jemina granted a **lease** of her flat to Umar for five years with a permission given to Umar to store coal in a shed in the garden of the building. In this situation, the **common law** would recognise an implied **grant** of an **easement**, i.e., right to store coal in the shed, to Umar. This is also known as **quasi-easement**. Similarly, if after the expiry of the five-year **lease** Jemina renewed it to Umar or leased or sold the flat to Avery (a third party) then the **statute** would recognise an implied **grant** of the **easement** to Avery. This is because the renewal of the **lease** or **grant** of a new **lease** or sale of the flat is a **conveyance**, the flat was under a **diversity of occupation** between Jemina (as a landlord) and Umar (as a **tenant**), and the right was not revoked.

8.3.1 Easements created by prescription

An **easement** can be created by **prescription**, i.e., by long usage. For instance, where an owner of a piece of land has enjoyed a 'right' over a land belonging to another for a long time then, if the 'right' is capable of being an **easement**, it may eventually become an **easement** simply through the long use of the right. This is a **legal** right. **Easements** created by **prescription** can only operate between **freeholders**. It is important for you to note that **easements** created by **prescription** must satisfy the general requirements for creating an **easement**.[8] Also, the claimant must show two things:

1. That his/her use has been of the appropriate nature, i.e., as of right (not by force) and continuous.
2. That s/he has acquired the right by one of the three methods of **prescription**:
3. **Prescription** at **common law** (20 years subject to rebuttable evidence of interruption by the **servient** landowner);
4. The doctrine of lost modern grant (20 years subject to rebuttable evidence of '**no grant**', this can be any 20 years so does not need to be immediately before the claim);
5. Statutory **prescription**.[9] The Prescription Act recognises 20 and 40 years of prescription as **easements**. The Act specifies how the periods of 20 and 40 years are to be measured – unlike lost modern grant it is not possible to choose any period that the claimant wishes. So, the 20 and 40 years must be the period next before

8 See the requirements discussed in Section 8.2.
9 The Prescription Act, 1832.

the claim.[10] In other words, the last 20 or 40 years of use. It is very important for you to note that, in order to make a claim based on 20 years of use under this Act the right must not be exercised secretly, forcefully, and with permission. If your claim is based on 40 years you would still need to prove that you have exercised the right for 40 years openly, without permission, and not forcefully. However, if your right began with a permission which later changed to 'without permission', this would not defeat your claim based on 40 years of use.

It is very important for you to remember that, in order to claim an **easement** right by **prescription** the use must be as of right (i.e. not enjoyed by force, secrecy, or permission), it must be continuous (this is obviously a matter of degree), and it must be in **fee simple** (i.e., by or on behalf of a fee simple owner against a fee simple owner). This is because the basis of a prescriptive claim is an immemorial user (since time immemorial) so an **easement** can only be prescribed for in respect of a **fee simple** estate.

Please also note that, as the rationale of the law of **prescription** lies in the acquiescence of the servient owner, s/he should not be bound by a kind of use (e.g. secret or infrequent) which s/he could not reasonably be expected to interfere with.

8.4 Extinguishment of easements

There is no statutory mechanism by which a person may apply for judicial termination of an **easement**. However, **easements** can extinguish in the following circumstances:

- When the **dominant** and **servient** land come under the ownership and possession (unification) of the same person.
- When the current owner of the **dominant land**:
  - Releases (expressly by **deed** or impliedly through conduct).
  - Abandons (20 years' non-use without explanation).
  - Terminates by Act of Parliament or judicial decision.
  - When it no longer benefits the dominant land.
- **Equitable easements** may also be void and unenforceable against subsequent purchasers of the **servient land** by reason of a failure to **register** (if required) in **registered** or **unregistered** land.[11]

8.5 Passing the benefits and burdens

Although **easements** are **proprietary** rights, this does not mean that they are automatically enforceable by third parties such as purchasers of the **dominant** and **servient** lands. The benefit of an **easement** will be enforceable by the purchaser of a

10 Ibid., S. 4.
11 For instances, where registration is required in registered and unregistered land, see Section 8.5.

dominant land, since it is a **proprietary** right, not a **personal** one. But the burden of an **easement** will only run with the land if the following criteria are fulfilled:

- **Legal easements**: All **legal easements** are interests that override a **first registration** of the servient land.[12] This is the case where the land was unregistered and now getting registered for the first time. **Legal easements** are expressly created after first registration so they must be entered on the register in order to exist, and once registered will bind all transferees of the **servient land**. Impliedly created **legal easements** may override if they are either known to or reasonably discoverable by, the purchaser, or have been used within a year before the purchase of the land.[13]
- **Equitable easements**: For **unregistered land**, **equitable easements** must be registered as Class D (iii) land **charge** in order to bind the new owner whether s/he goes for first registration or not. For **registered land**, **equitable easements** created after first **registration** is not protected by 'discoverable **actual occupation**'. Hence, it must be protected by an entry as a **notice** (**agreed** or **unilateral**) in the **register** of title of the **servient land**.

8.6 Profits à prendre

A *profit à prendre* is a right to take something from another's land. Such as wood, pasture, turf, or fish. A common example of a **profit** is where you have a right to fish or hunt in a public lake or land. This right gives you not only the right to fish or hunt but also to take any produces such as fish caught or wildlife hunted from there. Please note that you do not need a **dominant land** to enjoy a **profit**, but such land may exist. For instance, you may have a right to fish or hunt in your neighbouring lake or land but this right may also be available as a **profit** to others who are not neighbours of the owner of the lake or land.

Chapter revision points

- **Easements** are **proprietary rights** over a neighbouring land for the beneficial enjoyment of that land.
- An **easement** can be **legal** or **equitable**.
- The law of **easement** must accommodate the needs of the **dominant tenement** (benefited land) and must also ensure that the **servient tenement** (burdened land) does not become overburdened and inalienable.
- An **easement** must be capable of being an **easement** such as a right of way, parking. A **personal right** cannot be an **easement** such as a right to collect honey from a neighbour's land.

12 LRA 2002, para 3 of Sch. 1.
13 Ibid., para 3, Sch. 3.

- An **easement** can be created by **grant** and/or **reservation** – which can be **express** or **implied**.
- An **easement** can be created by **prescription**, i.e., by long use.
- Already-existing **easements** can be passed on as benefits and/or burdens under the **common law** and **statute**.
- An **easement** can be extinguished for reasons such as where both the **dominant** and **servient tenements** become under the ownership of the same person, when the **easement** no longer benefits the **dominant land**, a release by the **dominant** landowner, a lack of **registration**.
- Passing the benefit and burden of an **easement** depends on whether the **servient land** is **registered** or **unregistered**, and the applicable rule for registering the **easement**.
- **Profits** (*profits à prendre*) are rights to take a living or growing produce from somebody else's land. You do not need to be the owner of a **dominant land** to exercise these rights.

Multiple choice question

In 2012, Jemina, the registered freehold owner of a farm, granted certain rights *by deed*. Please identify which of the following grants are easements:

(a) Avery (a neighbour), the right to park her car in the car park of the farm.
(b) Bianca (another neighbour), the right to use the swimming pool on the farm in the afternoon of each and every weekend as she does not have a swimming pool on her land.
(c) Umar, the right to collect half a tonne of pineapples each and every year from the farm.
(d) Niamh (a neighbouring farmer who occupies land a few miles away), the right to store up to 15 tonnes of coal in the storage of the farm.
(e) Mohammad (not a neighbour), the right to store a tonne of hay in the main shed of the farm.

Answer: See Appendix C.

9 Freehold covenants

Chapter overview

Freehold covenants are promises made by a **deed** between **freehold** property owners where one party promises the other to do or not to do certain things on their land for the benefit of another neighbouring land. The land that benefits from the **covenant** is called 'the **benefited land**', and the land that bears the burden is called 'the **burdened land**'.

For instance, Jemina is the owner of a large manor house. She sold a converted barn, situated on the ground of the manor house, to Umar with the conditions that: (i) Umar must use the barn as a family home; (ii) he must not run a business from the barn; (iii) he must not build anything above 60 metres from the ground level; and (iv) he must maintain the garden. These conditions are **covenants** between two **freeholders** Jemina (the **covenantee** – who enjoys the benefit of a **covenant**) and Umar (the **covenantor** – who bears the burden of a **covenant**). In this setting, Jemina's retained manor house is the **benefited land** (indicated by a +), and Umar's converted barn is the **burdened land** (indicated by a –). See Figure 9.1.

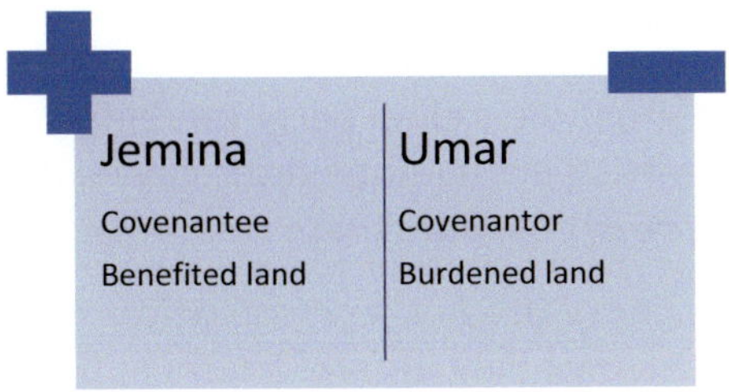

Figure 9.1 The covenantee and covenantor in a freehold covenant.

DOI: 10.4324/9781003204954-9

9.1 The nature of a freehold covenant

Covenants are **proprietary** obligations.[1] They are enforceable between the **covenantor** and **covenantee** irrespective of whether contractual **consideration** is given. Hence, **covenants** may be given in a standalone transaction by one neighbour to another or are more likely to arise when a person sells part of his/her land to another. The purpose of a **covenant** is to retain the benefit of a land so it cannot be affected by a new owner who purchased a piece of land carved out of the **benefited land**. The court recognised the remedy against a landowner who acquired a piece of land in the knowledge that it was affected by a **covenant**, even though it had been created by some other person.[2] Therefore, a new purchaser of a **burdened land** may be bound by a **covenant**. It is important for you to note that **covenants** may be negative (**restrictive**) or positive. For instance, a negative **covenant** is where it prohibits the **covenantor** from running a business on the property, and a positive **covenant** is where it binds the covenantor to do certain activities such as maintaining the garden.

9.2 Enforceability between the original parties

The original parties to a **covenant** can enforce it against each other under the rule of '**privity of contract**'. So, in the above example (see Figure 9.1), the **covenants** are binding between Jemina and Umar as original parties who created the **covenants** and agreed to be bound between themselves. This is a mutual obligation based on **privity of contract**. However, a **privity of contract** does not exist beyond the original parties. Therefore, the law that would apply to successors to a **covenantor** and a **covenantee** would depend on the rules of **common law** and **equity** (see below).

Please note that, in addition to the rules of **common law** and **equity**, a third party, who is not a party to the contract, can sue the **covenantor** under the Contract (Rights of Third Parties) Act 1999. A third party can be a new purchaser of a neighbouring land who would also benefit from the **covenant**, such as a covenant to maintain a garden, despite not being a party to the original contract between the **covenantor** and **covenantee**. In this situation, a third party can enforce a covenant **unless** the original parties to the contract did not intend the **covenant** to be enforceable by a third party. Section 1 of the Act provides that:

(1) Subject to the provisions of this Act, a person who is not a party to a contract (a 'third party') may in his own right enforce a term of the contract if:
   (a) the contract expressly provides that he may, or
   (b) subject to subsection (2), the term *purports to confer a benefit on him.*

1 For a discussion about the differences between a proprietary and personal right/obligation please see ch. 1.

2 *Tulk v Moxhay* [1848] 41 ER 1143.

(2) Subsection (1) (b) does not apply if on a proper construction of the contract *it appears that the parties did not intend the term to be enforceable by the third party.*

9.3 Enforceability against successor in title to the original covenantor

A **covenant** can be enforced not only against the original covenantor, but also against anyone who comes into possession or occupation of the land burdened by the covenant.[3] However, the following conditions, imposed by **common law** and **equity**, must be satisfied:

- **Common law**:
  - It will not pass a burden of any **covenants**.
  - The ways to circumvent the burden problem are limited and deficient.
  - We need **equity**'s help!
- **Equity**: Only the burdens of **restrictive covenants** (opposed to positive burdens) will pass.[4]

9.3.1 Passing the burden

As a burden of a **covenant** cannot pass in **common law**, it can only pass in **equity**. According to **equity**, only *burdens* of a ***restrictive*** *(negative)* ***covenant*** will pass.

In the above example (see Figure 9.1), if Umar sells his barn to Emily, the burdens of the negative **covenants** such as (i), (ii), and (iii) will pass on to her but not the positive covenant such as (iv).

Please note that **restrictive** (negative) **covenant** is a question of substance rather than form, so it is irrelevant how the covenant is actually worded. Hence, (i) is a negative covenant although it has been phrased in positive terms. Based on this, 'must use the barn as a family home' actually means that 'the barn must not be used for anything else except as a family home'. So, this is a negative **covenant**. Similarly, where a **covenant** was expressed as an obligation to positively keep the land as an open space – this was held rightly to be a negative **covenant** in substance because this was a **covenant** not to build.[5]

3 Ibid.
4 *Rhone v Stephens* [1994] 2 AC 310.
5 *Tulk v Moxhay* [1848] 41 ER 1143.

In addition to the above condition, i.e., **restrictive**/negative covenant, a **covenant** must touch and concern the land. This means that the **covenant** must affect the **burdened land** and/or benefit the **benefited land**. Generally, the following questions are being asked:

1. Could the **covenant** impose a burden on any owner of an **estate** in the land as opposed to the particular original owner?
2. Does the **covenant** affect the nature, quality, mode of user, or value of the burdened land?
3. Is the **covenant** actually expressed to be personal so that, irrespective of its substance, it is meant to operate only as a promise binding the original **covenantor**?

If the answer to the question (a) is yes, (b) is yes, and (c) is no, this will normally be taken by the court as being capable to touch and concern the land.[6]

The basic rule is that a **covenant** must have been imposed to benefit the land of the original **covenantee**. Hence, a **covenant** which was imposed to benefit anyone other than the original **covenantee** is not enforceable. However, there are a few exceptions to the basic rule. For instance, a covenant can validly benefit a third party such as a **lessor** (landlord) and a **mortgagor** (borrower) to protect their **proprietary** interest even though they are not the original **covenantee**. Similarly, a local authority may enforce a **covenant** against those persons deriving title under the **covenantor**, notwithstanding that the authority are not in possession of or interested in any land for the benefit of which the **covenant** was entered into, in like manner and to the like extent as if they had been in possession of or interested in such land, where:

1. A local housing authority have disposed of land held by them for any of the purposes of this Act and the person to whom the disposal was made has entered into a covenant with the authority concerning the land.
2. An owner of any land has entered into a covenant with the local housing authority concerning the land for the purposes of any of the provisions of this Act.[7]

This is very common where a local authority sold its land to a housing association or developer to build houses which the **covenantor** purchased.[8] In this situation, although the **covenant** was not imposed to benefit the land of the original **covenantee** (the council) as they may not have retained any land in the development, the **covenant** (such as not to run a business in the social housing estate) is binding as an exception to the principle that – a **covenant** must have been imposed to benefit the land of the original **covenantee**.

6 *Swift Investments v Combined English Stores* [1989] AC 632.
7 The Housing Act 1985, S. 609.
8 For further discussion see Section 9.5.

The burden of a **restrictive covenant** must be intended to run with the land. The intention can be shown in the wording of the **covenant** which can be found in the contract of sale. In the absence of an express wording to the contrary, the court can presume an intention to run with the land.[9]

Additional (**notice**) requirements must be complied with depending on whether the land is **registered** or **unregistered**. If the land is **registered**, a **covenant** must be entered in the **charges register** of the **burdened land** as a **notice** in order to be binding unless it is otherwise protected as an **overriding interest**. If the land is **unregistered**, the covenant should be registered as Class D (ii) land **charge** or failing this the **doctrine of notice** will apply.[10]

9.4 Enforceability by a successor in title to the original covenantee

An **original covenantee** can sue the **original covenantor** under the **privity of contract**. Also, s/he can sue a successor to the **original covenantor** (such as a purchaser) with respect to negative/**restrictive covenants**. This is because the **common law** recognises the passing of the benefit of a **covenant**.

For instance, in the example outlined in Figure 9.4a, Jack (a purchaser from Jemina) can sue Umar (the **original covenantor**) in law.

As stated above, the benefit of a **covenant** passes in law. As a result, only the **original covenantor** (the defendant) can be sued by the claimant (successor in title of the **covenantee**) in law (as shown in Figure 9.4a). However, if the **original covenantor** has sold or transferred his/her title then the burden of a **covenant** cannot pass on to the successor of the **original covenantor** because burdens do not pass in law (as discussed in Section 9.3). However, it is very important for you to know that only the burdens of negative **covenants** (restrictive) would pass in equity. Therefore, the burdens of positive **covenants** would not pass on to the successors of the **covenantor**.

For instance, in the example outlined in Figure 9.4b, Jack (a purchaser from Jemina) can sue Emily (a purchaser from the **covenantor**) in equity (but not in law) to enforce the negative **covenants** only such as 'must not run a business'

9 LPA 1925, S. 79.
10 For a discussion on the land charges and doctrine of notice, see Chapter 2 (unregistered Land law).

but not to enforce the positive covenants such as 'to maintain the garden'. This has been explained further below.

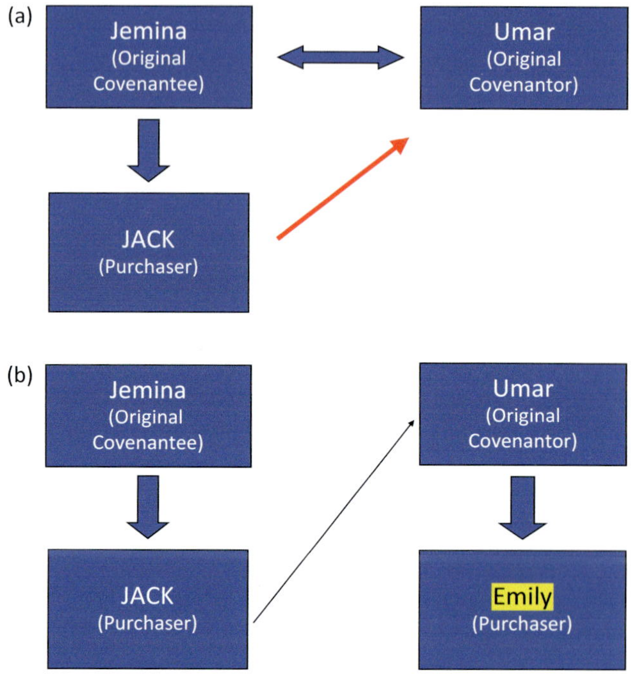

Figure 9.2 (a) Enforceability by Successors in Title in LAW. (b) Enforceability by Successors in Title in EQUITY.

9.4.1 Passing the benefit in law – Positive and negative covenants

In law, the benefit of both positive and negative **covenants** passes to a successor in tile to the **covenantee**. However, in order to enforce a negative or **restrictive covenant** the claimant (Jack, in our example) must sue the defendant (Emily) in **equity** because – a defendant is not liable to discharge a positive **covenant** but a negative one in **equity**. It is important for you to note that, in order to enforce a positive **covenant**, the claimant can only recourse to the *doctrine of mutual burden and benefit*. According to this doctrine, a positive **covenant**, i.e., to maintain the garden or fence, can be enforced if both the **covenantee** and **covenantor** (including their successors) can mutually benefit from such **covenant**. However, if both parties agreed to benefit from the covenant the **covenantor** could ask the covenantee to contribute to the expenses that would incur to fulfil the **covenant** such as paying the expenses to a gardener to carry out the maintenance work.[11] Also, a positive **covenant** can be

11 *Halsall v Brizell* [1957] Ch 169.

enforced against the **original covenantee**, in our example Umar, under the **common law**. However, it is important for you to note that if Umar has sold the property, it may not be possible to locate him so the possibility to enforce the covenant against him may turn out to be very remote.

Please note that irrespective of the nature of the **covenants** (positive or negative) a successor from the **covenantee** (the claimant) must have a **legal estate** in the **benefited land**. However, the claimant does not need to have the same **legal estate** as the original **covenantee**.[12] Thus, the **original covenantee** may have been the **freeholder**, but the claimant will succeed even if they have only a **legal lease**. Also, the benefit of the **covenant** must be annexed (also known as **annexation**) to a **legal estate** in the land, either expressly or by implication or by **statute**.[13] However, the following conditions must be fulfilled:

- The land is capable of benefiting from the **covenant**.
- The land to be benefited must be easily identified from the **covenant** and not only by extrinsic evidence.

Please note that a claimant can assign (also known as assignment) his/her right to sue to enforce a **covenant** to any person (such as a **lessee**) by giving notice in writing to the **covenantor**.

Please also note that under the Contract (Rights of Third Parties) Act 1999 – contracts after 11 May 2000 can benefit a non-party if the contract expressly provides, or purports to confer benefit on him/her. So, a third party who is neither a **covenantee** nor a **covenantor** can enforce a **covenant** where the **original covenantor** and **covenantee** expressly or impliedly conferred a benefit on him/her.

9.4.2 Passing the benefit in equity – Only negative covenant

As stated above, only the burden of a negative or **restrictive covenant** can pass in **equity**.[14] Based on this, the claimant can only sue to enforce the benefit of a negative **covenant**. The law cannot help the claimant to enforce a **positive covenant** as it does not allow this type of covenant to pass on to the successors in title. As stated in Section 9.4.1, in order to enforce a **positive covenant** the claimant can only recourse to the 'doctrine of mutual burden and benefit' and/or a remote possibility to enforce it against the **original covenantor** if s/he can be found.

12 LPA 1925, S. 78.
13 Ibid
14 See Section 9.3.1.

9.5 Scheme of development

Scheme of development is a building scheme where all purchasers acquire their properties from the same **vendor** (seller). This is very popular in areas where new-built properties are being sold to people by the same builder or building company. In this setting, the seller divides the entire estate to plots prior to the sales. The plots can also be identified in the planning permission. Once the plots are being divided, the seller imposes **covenants** for the benefit of all the plots. A common example of such a **covenant** is that 'the property cannot be used for anything else than a single-family home'. Every purchaser buys on the understanding that the **covenant** benefits all the other plots in the scheme.[15] A scheme of development is very common in modern development of **estates**. This is a unique example of where the **covenantee** (the building company/seller) does not need to retain any land/plot in order to impose a **covenant** on a **burdened land**. As a result, all the plots in a scheme are being benefited as well as burdened by the **covenants**. In this setting, a new buyer of a plot can claim a benefit under the **covenant** despite not being a party to the **original covenant** where the **vendor** intended the **restrictive**/negative covenant to continue for the benefit of all the plots.[16] It is important for you to note that in a scheme of development the plot owners cannot enforce a **positive covenant** against a new buyer who purchased a plot in the scheme. However, the doctrine of 'mutual benefit and burden' can be adopted here to address this issue as discussed above.[17]

9.6 Variation, termination, and removal of restrictive covenants

The Upper Tribunal has the power to vary or discharge or modify an existing **covenant**. The LPA 1925 provides that (**emphasis highlighted in bold and italics**), the Upper Tribunal shall (without prejudice to any concurrent jurisdiction of the court) have power from time to time, on the application of any person interested in any **freehold** land affected by any restriction arising under **covenant** or otherwise as to the user thereof or the building thereon, by order wholly or partially to discharge or modify any such restriction ... on being satisfied:

(a) that by reason of changes in the character of the property or the neighbourhood or other circumstances of the case which the Upper Tribunal may deem material, the ***restriction ought to be deemed obsolete***, or
(aa) that in a case falling within subsection (1A) below the continued existence thereof ***would impede some reasonable user of the land for public or private purposes*** ... or, as the case may be, would unless modified so impede such user; or

15 *Elliston v Reacher* [1908] 2 Ch 374.
16 LPA 1925, S. 56.
17 See Section 9.4.1; see also *Halsall v Brizell* [1957] Ch 169.

(b) that ***the persons of full age and capacity for the time being or from time to time entitled to the benefit of the restriction***, whether in respect of **estates** in **fee simple** or any lesser estates or interests in the property to which the benefit of the restriction is annexed, ***have agreed***, either expressly or by implication, by their acts or omissions, to the same being discharged or modified; or
(c) that the proposed discharge or modification ***will not injure the persons entitled to the benefit*** of the restriction.[18]

It is important for you to remember that, of all the statutory grounds, ground (aa) is the most often relied upon. This enables the Tribunal to discharge or modify a restriction if:

- The restriction impedes 'some reasonable user of land for public or private purposes'.
- In impeding that user, the restriction 'does not secure to persons entitled to the benefit of it any **practical benefits** of substantial value or advantage to them' OR 'is contrary to the **Public interest**'.
- 'That money will be an adequate compensation for the loss or disadvantage (if any) which any such person will suffer from the discharge or modification'.

It is very important for you to remember that the Upper Tribunal (UT) is very reluctant to allow claims of modifying or discharging an already-existing **restrictive covenant**. So, it is very difficult to successfully make a claim to modify or discharge a negative **covenant**. However, the UT may exercise its **discretion** to uphold a claim where there is a **practical benefit** to support that. For instance, where the character of the area has changed in recent years that the property cannot be restricted any longer to use as a family home only without denying a **practical benefit** to run a business there. This happens where the area has become a commercial hub in recent years so a **practical benefit** for the property would be to allow the current owner to run a business from there.

Chapter revision points

- **Covenants** are **proprietary** obligations. They are enforceable between the **covenantor** and **covenantee** irrespective of whether contractual **consideration** is given. **Covenants** may be given in a standalone transaction by one neighbour to another or is more likely to arise when a person sells part of their land to another.
- **Covenants** developed because courts of **equity** were prepared to **grant** a remedy against a landowner who acquired land in the knowledge that it was affected by a **covenant**, even though it had been created by some other person: *Tulk v Moxhay* (1848).
- **Covenants** may be negative (**restrictive**) or **positive**.

18 LPA 1925, S. 84 (1).

The passing of a benefit or burden depends on the rule of **common law** and **equity**.

- In **common law**:
    - Burdens do not pass.
    - Only benefits pass but five conditions must be fulfilled.
    - The benefits of both restrictive and positive covenants pass to the successors in title of the covenantee.
    - The **covenant** must touch and concern the burdened land.
    - The **covenant** must have been imposed to benefit land of the **original covenantee**.
    - The **covenant** must be intended to run with the land.
    - Additional (**notice**) requirement must be complied with depending on whether the land is **registered** or **unregistered**.
    - Only the **original covenantor** (the defendant) can be sued by a claimant (successor in title of the **covenantee**).
    - In **equity**:
    - The benefit of a **covenant** passes to the successors of a **covenantee**.
    - The burden of a **positive covenant** does not pass. So, the burden of a negative or **restrictive covenant** can only pass.
    - The burden of **restrictive covenants** will pass in **equity** if five conditions (stated above) are satisfied except the first condition because in equity only the burden of a restrictive covenant will pass.
- A scheme of development must fulfil the following criteria:
    - All purchasers acquire their property from the same **vendor**.
    - The **vendor** has divided the **estate** into plots prior to the sales.
    - The **restrictive covenants** were intended by the **vendor** to continue for the benefit of all the plots.
    - Every purchaser must acquire the plot in the understanding that the **covenants** benefit all the other plots in the scheme.
- A **third party** can enforce a **covenant** under the Contract (Rights of Third Parties) Act 1999 where the **original covenantee** and **covenantor** did not have a contrary intention.
- The Upper Tribunal has the statutory power to discharge or modify **restrictive covenants** affecting land.
- A **positive covenant** can be enforced under the principle of 'mutual benefit and burden'.

Multiple choice question

Acorn Builders Ltd owned a freehold land in London Road. They divided the land into three plots and sold them to three different buyers. Each transfer of the plots was by deed. The deed included a covenant which provided that 'the property must be used as a single private family home'. Umar recently purchased one of the plots and started to run his accountancy business from the property. Which of the following are CORRECT?

(a) Umar is not bound to comply with the covenant because he was not one of the parties who originally accepted it.
(b) Umar is not bound to comply with the covenant because it is a positive covenant which passed on to the successor in title.
(c) Umar is bound to comply with the covenant because the burden of a restrictive covenant passed on to him in equity.
(d) Umar is bound to comply with the covenant but he can make an application to the Upper Tribunal to discharge or modify the covenant as this is deemed to be obsolete.
(e) Umar can escape from his burden to comply with the covenant under the Contract (Rights of Third Parties) Act 1999.

Answer: See Appendix C.

10 Adverse possession

Chapter overview

This chapter addresses a very important right that may be created by **adverse possession**. This is also known as squatter's right. An adverse possessor can become an owner of a property, whether **registered** or **unregistered**, by possessing a piece of land against the consent or permission of the real owner. Therefore, the requirements for possession are namely, 'without force, without secrecy, and without permission'. The law has set up the period of time for which an adverse possessor would need to possess the land. It is important for you to note that the law of **adverse possession** for **registered** and **unregistered** land is not the same. This is because the law of adverse possession for **unregistered** and **registered** land is regulated by different **statutes**. For instance, whereas the Limitation Act 1980 applies to **adverse possession** of **unregistered land**, the Land Registration Act (LRA) 2002 applies to **registered land**. You will see later in the chapter that the LRA 2002 regime has limited the prospect of a successful claim of **adverse possession**.

10.1 What is adverse possession?

Adverse possession (AP) or squatter's right is an expression of a policy that denies the assistance of law to those who sleep on their rights, as well as ensures that there is an end to disputes concerning ownership of land. An adverse possession may arise where a squatter takes possession of a piece of land without the consent of the real owner and continues that possession without any interruptions or challenges from the real owner for a 'certain period of time'. Therefore, the requirements for possession are namely, 'without force, without secrecy, and without permission'. The 'certain period of time' has been set by the law.

For instance, in **unregistered land** an adverse possessor can become the real owner after 12 years of continuous possession.[1] On the other hand, in **registered**

1 Limitation Act 1980, S. 15.

DOI: 10.4324/9781003204954-10

land an adverse possessor can apply to become the **registered proprietor** of the land after 10 years of **adverse possession**.[2]

However, it is very important for you to note that an application to become the **registered proprietor** is very unlikely to be successful due to the obstacles that are being put in place by the LRA 2002.

10.2 How is adverse possession established?

From the above discussion, you can see that AP is possible in both **registered** and **unregistered** land. However, the nature and circumstances in which an AP can exist may differ. For instance, an AP can exist not only where a squatter enters a vacant property and continues to adversely possess that property but also where one neighbour adversely possesses some of the land of another neighbour by moving the fence between their respective lands.

For instance, Jemina is an owner of a house which has a back garden. Every five years Jemina put up a new fence in the boundary of her garden with that of her neighbour, Umar. In 2015, Jemina moved that fence about one metre into Umar's Garden. In this situation, Jemina can claim AP against Umar's land after completing the required period of **adverse possession** of that one metre of land.

The establishment of a claim of AP depends on if the property against which AP is claimed is an **unregistered land** or a **registered land**. However, there are certain substantive principles that apply to both **unregistered** and **registered** land. For instance, in order to make a valid AP claim in respect to either **registered** or **unregistered** land one must satisfy the following principles:

- **An intention to possess**: An intention by the adverse possessor to possess the land and to put it to his or her own use, whether or not s/he also knew that some other person had a claim or right to the land. This means that the adverse possessor does not need to know who the real owner is or what rights other people have on the land. All that is necessary is whether the adverse possessor has an intention to possess the land against any interest of the real owner only. S/he need not be concerned with any **third-party** rights such as right under an **estoppel**. Therefore, the adverse possessor must not be in possession with the consent or permission from the real owner or by force. For instance, a possession cannot be adverse where the real owner has permitted such possession

2 LRA 2002, S. 96, and Sch. 6.

expressly or impliedly, e.g., by a licence, or where the possessor has possessed the property by force.

- **Physical possession of the land**: The key criterion here is 'dispossession'. The adverse possessor must dispossess the real owner by taking physical possession of the land against the intention or permission of the real owner (aka the paper owner).[3]

10.3 Unregistered land

Where the land is **unregistered**, the law of limitation applies. Under this law, an adverse possessor must possess the land against the paper owner for the following period of time:

- 12 years from the moment of adverse possession.[4]
- 30 years where the owner is a sole **charitable corporation** (bishop).[5]
- 6 years for **joint tenancy** on the death of one of the joint tenants. However, 12 years against a **life tenant**.[6]

Please note that the above period of **adverse possession** must be continuous. A continuity may be broken and/or an **adverse possession** may be interrupted. This is known as 'stopping the clock'. A clock may stop to run and thereby an **adverse possession** could be interrupted on the following situations:

- On a successful action for possession or **declaration of title**.
- On an acknowledgment of title of the paper owner by adverse possessor.[7]
- On the retaking of custody and control by the paper owner of the land (without force).
- By permission given by the paper owner.

Please note that the continuous period of AP does not have to be all in one go or simultaneous. This means that two or more instances of **adverse possession** can be combined to make it 12 years.

> For instance, Jemina adversely possessed a house for six years. After that, she acknowledged the real owner's interest and remained there as a **tenant**. After two years, she stopped paying rent and wrote to the real owner that she was occupying the land as an adverse possessor. She continued this for another six years. Jemina can combine these two instances of 6 years' adverse possessions in order make it 12 years. Please note that this is only applicable to unregistered land.

3 *Pye v Graham* [2002] 3 WLR 221.
4 Limitation Act (LA) 1980, S. 15.
5 Ibid., Sch. 1, para 10.
6 LA 1980, S. 15.
7 LA 1980, S. 29, 30.

10.4 Registered land

Where the land is **registered**, no period of limitation applies.[8] Instead, the rules in LRA 2002 apply. An adverse possessor may apply to the **land registrar** to become the **registered proprietor** of the land once s/he has adversely possessed the land or property for ten years.[9] Unlike law, the adverse possession needs to be continuous. That means a claimant cannot combine two or more instances of adverse possessions to make it ten years.

As stated above, the LRA 2002 regime has made it almost impossible for adverse possessors or squatters to successfully make an AP claim. This is because the new system will alert **the registered proprietor** of any AP claim to which s/he can respond to safeguard his/her interest. However, if s/he fails to respond within two years from the receipt of the alert s/he may lose title (initially) but with an option that would remain open for him/her to make an application for **rectification** of the **register** and recover title if the **adverse possession** claim is proven to be false.[10] Therefore, the right of AP in **registered land** is not automatic but subject to making a successful application to the **Land Registry** which is likely to be challenged by the paper owner.

Please note that, if a real owner sells his/her land after knowing that the AP has applied for **registration** the entitlement to be registered as the new owner is enforceable against:

- A purchaser of the land from the current **registered proprietor** if the adverse possessor is in discoverable **actual occupation** of the land.[11]
- A transferee who is not a purchaser.[12] For instance, a person who received the property as a gift or by succession.

As a result, a new buyer of a **registered land** who is a subject to an AP application is not bound by the AP's right unless the latter is in **actual occupation** that is discoverable after careful inspection, or the former is a recipient of a gift or an **inheritance**.

Once an application for **registration** has been made by the AP, the **registered proprietor** or the paper owner has the following options:

- **Option 1**: Consent or agree to the application. However, this is very unlikely.
- **Option 2**: Object to the application. In case of an objection, the parties can settle the dispute between themselves or refer to the **registration** division of the Property Chamber of the First Tier Tribunal for a decision.

8 LRA 2002, S. 96.
9 LRA 2002, Sch. 6.
10 *Baxter v Mannion* [2011] 1 WLR 1594.
11 LRA 2002, Sch. 3, para 2.
12 LRA 2002, S. 28.

- **Option 3**: Serve a counter-notice to defeat the application. However, on receipt of a counter-notice the adverse possessor must satisfy one of the following **exceptions**:
  - **Exception 1**: **Estoppel**, **unconscionabl**y, and ought to be registered (*discretionary remedy*): an **estoppel** can be claimed against the **registered proprietor** in respect to a counter-notice where the squatter has built a structure on the land of the **registered proprietor** in the mistaken belief that s/he was the owner of it and the proprietor knowingly acquiesced his mistaken belief. The court can also exercise its **discretion** to **register** the squatter as a registered proprietor where a contract of sale between him/her and the registered proprietor (seller) failed due to not taking any steps by the former to complete the purchase.
  - **Exception 2**: The squatter/adverse possessor is, for some other reason, entitled to be registered as proprietor. For instance:
    - Where the squatter is a **beneficiary** under a **trust**.
    - Where the squatter was a buyer and paid the purchase price but to whom the land was never transferred.
  - **Exception 3**: The boundary exception (*physical features vs title plan*). In this exception, the counter-notice would not be enforceable where:
    - The applicant's land is adjacent to that to which the claim relates (disputed land).
    - The exact boundary has not been determined.
    - The disputed land has been registered for more than one year.
    - At least ten years of adverse possession have been completed and the applicant reasonably believed that the disputed land belonged to him/her.[13]

It is important for you to note that, if none of the above options is exercised or failed, then the **registered proprietor** will have two years to recover possession of the land. If s/he fails to recover possession, then the adverse possessor may reapply within another two years – when s/he will become a **registered proprietor**. However, please note that there is no settled rule about how many times or years such reapplication can be made. The Law Commission has made a proposal in 2018 to limit it to ten years but the government has not implemented this at the date of writing.

10.5 The impact of human rights on adverse possession

The human rights of both the landowner and adverse possessor are being considered in this section. Dispossessing a paper owner or refusing to register a squatter's right

13 *Zarb v Parry* [2011] EWCA Civ 1306.

may result in a violation human rights such as 'a right to respect for one's private and family life, his home and his correspondence'.[14] However, the European Court of Human Rights (ECtHR) recognised that

> *adverse possession is a proportionate and legitimate response to a public interest concerning the need to limit claims in relation to land and a landowner cannot plead a violation of their right to property under Article 1 Protocol of the Convention if they 'lose' their title to an adverse possessor.*[15]

Similarly, the court recognised that squatting is a **trespass** but held that it would be rare for their removal to be so disproportional as to be contrary to Article 8.[16]

10.6 The relationship between trespass and adverse possession

The relationship between **trespass** and **adverse possession** has been reviewed recently by the parliament. Because **adverse possession** is an act of **trespass** (which is a civil wrong and a criminal office too) it was argued that a trespasser should not be entitled to become a **registered proprietor** or owner of a land into which they trespassed. This is because no one should be able to legally make a gain by their illegal act, i.e., trespass. As a result of this, the legality of the right created by **adverse possession** was challenged. Due to this, trespassing was made a criminal act.[17] Since then, the question arose – can a person (a squatter) make a successful claim to a title based on what might be an unlawful act of trespass? The court of appeal answered, yes. It held that 'commission of a criminal offence is not itself a bar to achieving title **by adverse possession**'.[18]

Chapter revision points

- **Adverse possession** is an expression of a policy that denies assistance of law to those who sleep on their rights, as well as ensuring that there is an end to disputes concerning ownership of land.
- Different laws apply to AP with respect to **unregistered land** and **registered land**.
- In **unregistered** land, a 12-year period of AP automatically gives the adverse possessor a right to become the paper owner.

14 ECHR, Art. 8.
15 *Pye v UK* (2007) 46 EHRR 45.
16 *Malik v Fassenfelt* [2013] EWCA Civ 798.
17 Legal Aid, Sentencing, and Punishment of Offenders (LASPO) Act 2012, S. 144.
18 *Best v Chief Land Registrar* [2015] EWCA Civ 17.

- In **registered** land, a ten-year period of AP only gives the adverse possessor the right to apply to become a **registered proprietor**. However, making an application may not be successful due to the **statutory** barriers that are in place. As a result, it is very difficult for an AP to become a registered proprietor.
- Dispossession of the real owner or the squatter is a question of human rights. However, the EctHR decided that placing statutory barriers to deprive a squatter is not a violation of Article 8 ECHR (private and family life).
- S. 144 of LASPO 2012 (came into effect on 1 September 2012) has made trespassing in a residential property a criminal offence but the court held that 'commission of a criminal offence is not itself a bar to achieving title by adverse possession'.

Multiple choice question

Which of the following positions, in relation to adverse possession, are legally CORRECT?

(a) An adverse possessor will have to complete 12 years of adverse possession in order to become a paper owner if the disputed land is registered.
(b) An adverse possessor will have to complete 12 years of adverse possession in order to become a paper owner if the disputed land is unregistered.
(c) An adverse possessor will have to complete ten years of adverse possession in order to make an application to become the registered proprietor if the disputed land is registered.
(d) An adverse possessor will have to complete ten years of adverse possession in order to make an application to become the registered proprietor if the disputed land is unregistered.
(e) Irrespective of the nature of the disputed land, i.e., registered or unregistered, an adverse possession claim must establish that they have completed 12 years of adverse possession.

Answer: See Appendix C.

11 Mortgages

Chapter overview

A **mortgage** is a **conveyance** of land as a security for the payment of debt or discharge of some other obligation.[1] It is quite common for people to borrow money from a bank to buy properties. When money is borrowed by giving the house as a security for the debt, the transaction is called a **mortgage**. A **mortgage** is a **legal** interest.[2] There are two parties in a **mortgage**, namely the **mortgagor** or borrower and **mortgagee** or the lender.

This chapter will discuss the essential characteristics of a **mortgage**, different types of **mortgages** that can be created, rights and remedies available to the **mortgagor** and **mortgagee**, and mortgage fraud and professional conduct.

11.1 The characteristics of a mortgage

As stated above, a **mortgage** is a device for the purchase of a property by borrowing money from the **mortgagee** in exchange for giving the property as a security for the debt. However, there are two essential characteristics of a **mortgage**, such as:

- A contract between a borrower and lender.
  - The **mortgagor** will enter into a binding contract with the **mortgagee** whereby a capital sum will be lent on the security of property owned by the **mortgagor**.
  - The parties (**mortgagor** and **mortgagee**) to a **mortgage** are subject to contractual obligations. Hence, if the **mortgagor** fails to make repayments the **mortgagee** can sue the former on contract for repayment of the loan, plus interest and costs.[3]
- An interest in land in its own right.
  - A **mortgage** is a **proprietary** interest in the land over which it takes effect. However, the borrower retains an 'equity of redemption', i.e., the right to

1 *Santley* v *Wilde* [1899] 2 Ch 474.
2 LPA 1925, S. 1 (2).
3 *Alliance & Leicester* v *Slayford* [2001] 3 HLR 743.

DOI: 10.4324/9781003204954-11

redeem the **mortgage** debt by the **mortgagor** even after defaulting to make repayments. This can happen where the **mortgagor** initially defaulted due to losing his/her job but later on got another job which re-enabled him to make repayments.

11.2 Types of mortgages

There are mainly **four** different types of **mortgage**s. These are repayment mortgage, endowment mortgage, current account mortgage, and charge. Each of these are explained below:

- **Repayment mortgage**: Frequently used for the purchase of residential property and to finance commercial activities. Both the capital and interest are paid back in instalments, with usually the early instalments representing pure interest, and the later instalments comprising a greater capital element.
- **Endowment mortgage**: Only the interest is paid back in monthly instalments. However, the **mortgagor** enters into an 'endowment policy' which normally guarantees enough money to pay off the capital sum. However, if there is any shortfall then **mortgagor** is responsible for that.
- **Current account mortgage**: An overdraft facility in a current account is used to purchase property. In this type of **mortgage**, an overdrawn facility is attached to the account which the borrower uses to purchase the property. Although the borrowed amount is an overdraft facility it is the mortgaged property that is secured against the borrowing.
- **Charge**: A **charge** of property or a **charge** by **deed** by way of legal **mortgage**.[4] In this type of **mortgage**, a **charge** is created over the mortgaged property in a **deed** and then **registered**.

11.3 Creation of mortgages

The way **mortgages** are created has been changed significantly by **statutes**. Since 1925, the lender (**mortgagee**) no longer retains any interest in the property secured, instead the borrower (**mortgagor**) retains the fullest interest in the property. As a result, the borrower no longer conveys all the interests in the property to the **mortgagee**. The only interest a **mortgagee** has over the property subject to a **mortgage** is a '**charge**' which is an interest to recover the debt.

Mortgages may be **legal** or **equitable** depending on the ways they have been created. Whereas a **legal mortgage** is protected as a **charge**, an **equitable mortgage** is only protected as an equitable right which means that if there are two mortgages found in respect to a property where one is legal and the other is equitable the legal

4 LRA 2002, S. 23(1).

mortgage shall prevail. Therefore, a legal mortgage takes priority over an equitable mortgage.

11.3.1 Legal mortgages

A **legal mortgage** must be created by a **charge** by **deed** by way of **legal mortgage**. This means that a legal mortgage must be created by **deed** for **unregistered** land.[5] In the case of **registered** land, whether **freehold** or **leasehold**, a **deed** as well as registration of the **charge** is necessary.[6]

Once the **charge** is executed by the **mortgagor**, it must be substantially registered as a 'registered **charge**' against the registered title in order to take effect as a **legal mortgage**.[7] Once the **registration** is completed by the **mortgagee** it gives them a priority right over the charge.[8]

For instance, an **equitable mortgagee** could lose his/her priority over the land because of subsequent sale of the mortgaged **estate**, either by a **deed** in **unregistered conveyancing** or by a properly registered sale in **registered conveyancing**.

Registration also guarantees the validity of the **charge** even if there might have been some problems in the process such as where the borrower's signature was forged.[9]

11.3.2 Equitable mortgages

A **mortgage** may be **equitable** because:

- The borrower originally has only an **equitable** interest in the land.
- The borrower has an interest, but the **mortgage** has not been executed with the formality required by **statute** for the creation of a **legal** interest. For instance, it has not been **registered**.[10]

In addition to the priority of the **legal mortgage** over **equitable** ones as stated above, an **equitable mortgage** suffers from another very important disadvantage compared to a **legal mortgage**. For instance, in an **equitable mortgage** the **conveyance** transfers the entire **equitable interest** of the **mortgagor** in the property to the **mortgagee**. It is important for you to note that an **equitable mortgage** must be created in writing

5 LPA 1925, S. 1(2).
6 LRA 2002, S. 23(1), and 51.
7 LRA 2002, S. 25, 27.
8 LRA 2002, S. 29.
9 *Swift 1st v Chief Land Registrar* (2015) Ch 602.
10 LRA 2002, S. 27.

and signed by the parties.[11] Please also note that a **deed** is not necessary but essential in order for the **mortgagee** to import the power of sale in the event of default.[12]

Equitable mortgages are also known as informal mortgages. Where a **mortgage** was not created by **deed** or **registration** was not completed the **mortgage** transaction may suffer from errors, omissions, negligence, or fraud. Therefore, *a written document is the minimum requirement* for a **mortgage** to be valid. If there is no **deed** or specifically enforceable written contract then the **mortgage** will be void in both **law** and **equity**,[13] unless it could be saved by the doctrine of **proprietary estoppel**.[14]

Please note that there are situations where the court has an **equitable** jurisdiction to recognise a **mortgage** which is otherwise void. For instance, where not recognising a **mortgage** would be **unconscionable**. This is a common situation where one of the parties have been subjected to a representation which they relied on and as a result suffered loss.

For instance, if a borrower borrowed money by fraudulently representing that the borrowing was a personal loan where the money borrowed was paid to buy a property the court can exercise its **discretion** to give effect a **mortgage** as otherwise it would be **unconscionable** for the lender.[15]

If an **equitable mortgage** exists over **unregistered** land, it is registrable as a Class C(iii) land **charge**. If not so registered as a land charge under this category, the **mortgage** will be void against any purchaser of a **legal** or **equitable** interest in the land.[16]

In **registered** land, an **equitable mortgagee** should seek to protect his/her **mortgage** by means of an entry of a **notice** (agreed notice) against the **registered** title of the **mortgaged** property. A **restriction** may also be entered to alert the **mortgagee** of any proposed dealings with the **legal** title by the **mortgagor**.

11.3.3 Unregistered land

If the land is **unregistered**, the following types of **mortgages** are registrable as land **charges** under the LCA 1972:

11 LPA 1925, S. 53 (1); and LP (MP) A 1989, S. 2.
12 LPA 1925, S. 101 (1).
13 *United Bank of Kuwait v Sahib* [1997] Ch 107.
14 Proprietary estoppel has been discussed in Chapter 7.
15 *Kinane v Alimamy Mackie-Conteh* [2005] EWCA Civ 45.
16 LCA 1972, S. 2 and 4.

- A **puisne mortgage** (i.e., a legal mortgage not protected by deposit of deeds – the first **legal mortgagee** will normally hold the title deeds, as s/he is entitled to do so) as a Class C(i) land **charge**.
- A contract for a **legal mortgage** (an **estate contract**) as a Class C(iv) land **charge**.
- A **general equitable charge** as a Class C(iii) land **charge**.[17]

11.4 Mortgagor's right to the Equity of redemption

Equity of redemption is a unique and very important right for the borrower. It gives the borrower an **equitable** right to redeem the mortgage even after defaulting in making repayments. When a borrower fails to keep up repayments the lender mostly wants to sell the mortgaged property. However, the **equity** of redemption stops the lender from doing that without applying for permission to recover the mortgaged property (also known as ***foreclosure***). Once an application for **foreclosure** is approved by the court the lender can sell the property in order to recover the debt. Therefore, **equity** of redemption operates as a protector for the borrower from abuse and unfair treatment by the lender such as it prevents the lender from buying the mortgaged property. It is important for you to note that **foreclosure** is very rare in modern Land law practice as it is seen as a very draconian remedy.

11.5 Mortgagee's rights and remedies for default by the mortgagor

In case of any default to make repayments by the **mortgagor**, there are different types of remedies available to the **mortgagee**. Depending on the nature of default, these remedies are effective ways to pursue the best remedy available. For instance, if the borrower's default is temporary in nature, then the **mortgagee** may find it suitable to recover unpaid interests only until the borrower becomes able to regain their financial ability to make repayments of both the capital and interests. However, if the default is a long-term one or permanent in nature the **mortgagee** may find a recovery of the entire loan and termination of the **mortgage** more suitable.

The most common remedy that **mortgagees** pursue is an action on the contract for recovery of the debt. As a **mortgage** is a contract between the **mortgagor** and **mortgagee**, on default of payment the **mortgagee** can sue the **mortgagor** for breach of their express promise to repay the debt. This remedy can be sought by the **mortgagee** on the date of redemption, i.e., a date where the debt has to be repaid. As most **mortgage** repayments are made monthly, the **mortgagee** agrees to defer the remedy pending the payment of instalments. As a result, the lender can wait for a few months before seeking this remedy. Please note that this is a remedy where

17 LCA 1972, S. 2(4).

the **mortgagee** seeks to recover the full outstanding debt. This remedy can be very useful where a sale of the **mortgage** property fails to raise enough money to pay off the outstanding **mortgage** debt and the **mortgageor** has additional assets to meet the remaining liability. Therefore, this may not be a suitable remedy where the **mortgagor** is bankrupt. It is important for you to note, however, that any shortfall in sale price is not irrecoverable by a **mortgagee** because s/he is entitled to pursue the **mortgagor** for any amount outstanding after possession and sale for up to 12 years after the right to receive the money accrued but there are costs associated with this and a **mortgagor** may be unable to pay in any event.

Another very important remedy available to the **mortgagee** is the 'power of sale'. This power arises from the **mortgage** contract which expressly and impliedly confers a power to the **mortgagee** to sell the mortgaged property in case of default.[18] This remedy is available to recover the whole sum owed. This power is available to exercise on default of an instalment payment. However, before exercising this power of sale the **mortgagee** must do the following:

1. Serve a notice to the **mortgagor** requiring payment of the whole outstanding balance on the **mortgage**.
2. Three months need to pass since the issue of the notice and no payment was made within these three months.
3. The interests under the **mortgage** remained unpaid for two months.
4. The **mortgagor** breached some provisions of the **mortgage** as provided in the deed, i.e., letting out the mortgaged property without permission.[19]

It is important for you to note that before exercising the power of sale the **mortgagee** would want to exercise their right to possession of the mortgaged property in order to facilitate the sale. However, a right to possession can be challenged in court by the **mortgagor** if they can establish that the property is residential, and they can make some payments within a reasonable period of time.[20]

Please note that the remedies available on default in respect to an **equitable mortgage** is very similar to that of a **legal mortgage**.

> For instance, like a legal mortgage a default in an equitable **mortgage** can be remedied by exercising the right to sue on contract. However, there are certain reservations in respect to other rights such as 'power of sale'. In an **equitable mortgage**, a power of sale is only available when the mortgage is created by **deed**.

18 LPA 1925, S. 101(1).
19 LPA 1925, S. 103.
20 Administration of Justice Act 1970, S. 36.

Please note that a sale by an **equitable mortgagee** does not convey a **legal** title of the property to the purchaser.

11.5.1 Amendment to possession proceedings by the mortgagee

The law has recently changed to address the balance of protection between the **mortgagor** and **mortgagee**. The changes concern **mortgage** possession proceedings:

- First, from 1 April 2014, the powers under the Consumer Credit Act (CCA) 1974, part 9, has applied to regulate mortgage contracts under the FSMA (Financial Services and Markets Act 2000). It therefore follows that, for example, the CCA provisions relating to **time orders** apply to regulated **mortgage** contracts.
- Second, from 21 March 2016, most residential **mortgages** (including second mortgages) were brought within the scope of regulation under the FSMA 2000.

The above changes have brought in greater powers by the court in possession proceedings. Possession proceedings are claims made in court where a **mortgagee** applies for possession of the mortgaged property due to the **mortgagor's** default in making repayments. It replaced the application of the Administration of Justice Act (AJA) 1970 where the court had the power to adjourn, stay, suspend or postpone a possession order, only where it 'appear[ed] to the court that in the event of its exercising the power the **mortgagor** [was] likely to be able within a reasonable period to pay any sums due under the mortgage'.[21] As a result, the AJA provision solely focused on *the mortgagor's ability to repay* any sums due within a reasonable period. As a result, it avoids any attempt to measure what is truly valuable, valuing instead only that which is measurable, i.e., economic interests are readily quantifiable as opposed to social interests, e.g., loss of home, impact on the health and well-being of the household concerned and the community around them. However, it is very important for you to know that the new legal regime under the CCA has brought in new powers for the court.[22] For instance, the court now has the power to make a **time order**, as well as to suspend any possession order on terms and, where appropriate, to vary the terms of the mortgage agreement. Unlike the previous regime under the AJA, this process under the CCA does not exclude the consideration of interests beyond the economic ones. Therefore, it allows the judge to weigh both social and economic interests in determining the question of possession. It is important for you to note that, under the new regime, second mortgagors can no longer seek direct action under the CCA 1974 but rather must now rely on a complaint to the Financial Ombudsman Service (FOS) or a private action for damages under the FSMA 2000.

Under both AJA and CCA, the court has **discretion** to effectively suspend possession of the mortgaged property provided that the **mortgagor** keeps to the payment

21 AJA 1970, S. 36.
22 CCA 1974, part 9.

terms stipulated by the court. Therefore, the court is unlikely to exercise its **discretionary** power where a **mortgagor** does not have the means to repay at least some of what is owed hence the **mortgagee's** economic concerns remain a priority. Whereas the AJA is based entirely on an 'if you can pay, you can stay' approach with possession determined solely by what the borrower can afford, the CCA is based on what is just, taking into account the interests and positions of both parties including the means of the **mortgagor**. Additionally, the 'reasonable period' under the AJA rarely extends to the 'remaining term of the mortgage' for a number of reasons, not least that the judiciary's concern to ensure that the **mortgagee** should not have to wait for a disproportionately long time for contractually agreed payments to be honoured. However, under the CCA, 'the court retains a wide **discretion** in deciding the period of repayment—not being limited to a "reasonable period" as under the AJA provisions'. Another important point for you to note is that, under the AJA the court does not have the ability to alter the interest rate charged under the agreement, whereas under the CCA, such a power exists which has been exercised occasionally to reduce the interest rate to nil. However, please note that neither AJA 1970 nor CCA 1974 is open to a **mortgagor** who does not currently have the means to repay at least some of what is owed, hence the **mortgagee's** economic concerns still are priority.

11.6 Mortgage fraud and professional conduct

Mortgage fraud has been identified as a contentious issue in the property market. The Council of Mortgage Lenders has revealed that **mortgage** fraud has been estimated by the National Fraud Authority to amount to a total of over £1 billion annually.[23] **Mortgage** fraud can be committed in different and innovative ways, but the most common examples are:

- Misrepresentation of income or property value to obtain greater loans than a person is eligible.
- Overvaluing properties, using false identities, and failing to make any **mortgage** repayments.
- False/exaggerated **mortgage** applications.
- Fictitious borrowers.
- Several loans obtained from different lenders on the same property (also known as 'shotgunning').
- Inflated purchase price/failure to disclose incentives.
- Failure to disclose information where there is a legal duty to disclose.[24] If you are a **conveyancer**, failure to disclose a suspicious activity is an offence. Your duty

23 The Council of Mortgage Lenders Report (August 2013).
24 Fraud Act 2006.

to disclosure owed to the lender as well as public bodies such as the National Crime Agency.

- Value of a **mortgage** obtained through fraud is the proceeds of crime.[25]

As a solicitor you must verify the borrower's identity, disclose and report any suspicious activity to the lender as well as any crime prevention agencies. Please remember that you have a 'duty of confidentiality' to your client which requires you to keep their personal information, including financial information, confidential. However, this duty is subject to another overriding duty to prevent crime. The SRA Handbook requires a solicitor to disclose client's confidential information where this would protect the national security or prevent crime.[26] Also, the Law Society's Mortgage Fraud Practice Note states that 'you are only released from your duty of confidentiality where you are satisfied of a strong prima facie case that the client, or third party, was using you to further a fraud or other criminal purpose'.[27]

Please also note that **conveyancing** is a 'regulated activity'.[28] The law prohibits carrying on of a 'regulated activity' within the UK unless the person carrying out the activity is 'authorised' by the Financial Conduct Authority (FCA) or is 'exempt'. The Law Society is a 'Designated Professional Body' (DPB) that supervises and regulates 'exempt regulated activities' undertaken by solicitors' firms who are not authorised. Even where an activity is within the DPB regime it may be best to refer the client to an independent adviser who is authorised by the FCA or exempt.

Solicitors must identify 'conflict of interests' between clients.[29] The SRA Handbook states that as a solicitor you do not act if you have a conflict of interest or a significant risk of such a conflict. There are a few exceptions, such as (a) you can act as a solicitor where the clients have substantially common interest, i.e., common financial interest of the lender and borrower in a mortgage transaction; (b) you can also act where the client has competing interest (such as where some confidential information gives rise to a significant risk of a conflict) but they have given informed consent, you have put effective safeguards to protect their confidentiality, and you are satisfied that it is reasonable for you to act.[30]

> An example of such a situation is where you are acting as a solicitor for an unmarried couple to buy a family property and one of them told you that they are having a clandestine affair.[31]

25 Proceeds of Crime Act 2002.
26 SRA Code of Conduct 2019, para 6.3.
27 Law Society's Mortgage Fraud Practice Note, para 6.2
28 The Financial Services and Markets Act 2000.
29 *Royal Bank of Scotland v Etridge (No.2)* [2001] 4 All ER 449.
30 SRA Code of Conduct 2019, para 6.2.
31 *First Plus Financial Group plc v Hewett* [2010] EWCA Civ 312.

It is important for you to know that it is very common for a solicitor to give undertakings. An undertaking is a promise given by the solicitor to do or not to do something. For instance, promise to hold title **deeds** to the lender's order, to repay a bridging loan from net sale proceeds, to discharge the seller's **mortgage** in respect to the property sold, about exchange of contracts. The effects of giving an undertaking are that (a) it is personally binding on the solicitor; (b) it can be enforced by the court; and (c) a solicitor who fails to honour a professional undertaking is ***prima facie*** guilty of professional misconduct.[32]

Chapter Revision Points

- A **mortgage** is a contract between the **mortgageor** and **mortgagee** as well as an interest in land in its own right.
- There are mainly four different types of **mortgages**, namely repayment mortgage, endowment mortgage, current account mortgage, and **charge**.
- The only permissible method of creating a **legal mortgage** of registered **freehold** or **leasehold** estate is 'charge by deed by way of legal mortgage'.
- If the land is **unregistered**, the mortgages are registrable as land **charges** under the LCA 1972, which is a separate system from **registered** land.
- Mortgages can be **legal** or **equitable** depending on how they are created.
- Although the remedies available to the **mortgagees** after default under a **legal** and/or **equitable mortgage** are the same, the effect of those remedies are not.
- The CCA has brought in a wider **discretion** for the judges by replacing the AJA. For instance:
  - The court can, if it considers just, order the debtor to pay 'any sum owed under a regulated agreement ... by such instalments, payable at such times, as the court, having regard to the means of the debtor ... considers reasonable': CCA 1974 S. 129(2).
  - In addition, the court may also, tag on to a **time order** 'such provision as it considers just for amending any agreement or security in consequence of a term of the order': CCA 1974 S. 136. This is based on what is just, taking into account the interests and positions of both parties, including the means of the **mortgagor**. This has a potential therefore to allow for the inclusion of non-economic concerns as opposed to economic ones, and for both to be weighed against each other. Therefore, there is potential for the **mortgagors** who would not qualify for relief under the AJA 1970 to avail themselves of a **time order** by indicating an ability to repay the debt over a longer period and at a lower rate of interest.

32 *Rooks Rider v J.R. Steel* [1993] 4 All ER 716.

- Mortgage fraud is a serious concern, and solicitors as well as conveyancers have legal duties to address this.
- Solicitors have the duty to keep their clients' personal and financial information confidential, but this is subject to an overriding duty to disclose and report suspicious activities to crime prevention agencies.
- Solicitors also have the duty to avoid any conflict of interest between clients (whether borrower and lender).
- Solicitors can give undertakings which are legally binding and enforceable in courts. A breach of an undertaking can lead to professional misconduct.

Multiple Choice Question

Which of the following are CORRECT when a mortgagor of a residential property defaulted to make repayments?

(a) The mortgagee can sell the property straightaway to recover the outstanding debt.
(b) The mortgagee will have to send a written notice of default to the mortgagor and cannot sell the mortgaged property until three months passed since the notice was issued and no payments were made.
(c) The mortgagee would need to bring a possession proceeding before selling the mortgaged property.
(d) In a possession proceeding the court cannot take into account the social and economic interests of the mortgagor in determining the question of possession.
(e) In a possession proceeding the court can take into account the social and economic interests of the mortgagor under the Consumer Credit Act 1974.

Answer: See Appendix C.

Appendix A
Summary of cases

Chapter 2: Unregistered Land law

Doctrine of Notice: Kingsnorth Finance Co. Ltd v Tizard *[1986] 1 WLR 783*

The case illustrates the meaning of constructive and imputed notice. It also sheds light on what amounts to an 'actual occupation', which is relevant to registered land. It is important for you to note that although this case was decided on 'unregistered land' the decision is still relevant to understand actual occupation with respect to registered land.

Facts: Unmarried couple bought a house (unregistered land) in 1960. They got married in 1966. They had two children. The marriage broke down in 1982. In 1983, the husband applied for a mortgage without disclosing that he was not the sole owner. On a Sunday, a surveyor came to inspect the property and found evidence of a woman living there. He was told that the wife left a few months ago and she now lives at a nearby place. The mortgage broker appointed the surveyor. The surveyor prepared a valuation report in which he said that the premises were occupied by the 'applicant, son, and daughter' and that no tenancies were clear on inspection. The mortgage application was successful. However, the husband migrated to another country with the children.

Issue: Whether the charge (mortgage) was subject to the wife's equitable interest.

The outcome: When the matter went to court, the court decided that the surveyor Mr Marshall had constructive notice of the wife's interest and that the finance company thereby had imputed notice of Mrs Tizard's equitable interest. So why did the surveyor have constructive knowledge? Well, the judge thought that not all reasonable inspections and inquiries had been made and if they had been made, then they could have led to the discovery of Mrs Tizard's right. Why did the judge think this? Well firstly because of the discrepancy between what Mr Tizard had originally said about his marital status and what he said when Mr Marshall came to survey the property. This, the judge thought, should have put Mr Marshall on alert to find out more about the wife or whether she in fact had interest in the property. And so too should the fact of the children living there have alerted Mr Marshall to make further

DOI: 10.4324/9781003204954-12

inquiries. Additionally, the judge said that the inspection itself was insufficient because Mr Marshall should not have gone to the property at a pre-arranged time.

The judge decided that the surveyor did not make adequate inquiries and inspections which would otherwise have led to the discovery of Mrs Tizard's interest. A further point of interest in the judgement is that the judge did not think that the inspection needed to go as far as opening drawers and cupboards. And why did Kingsnorth have imputed notice? Because Mr Marshall was an agent of Kingsnorth. Therefore, anything he had known or was treated as having had notice of was automatically imputed to Kingsnorth, his employer. In conclusion, Kingsnorth was held to be bound by Mrs Tizard's equitable interest under a trust. In practice this meant that she kept her half-share of the value of the property. She could resist Kingsnorth's application for possession and when the house was sold, she was entitled to half of the proceeds. Kingsnorth could only look to the remaining half to get back what it was owed.

Land charges registration requirement: Diligent Finance Company v Alleyne *(1971) 23 P & CR 346*

Case summary: Registration against the wrong name was made in this case. In this case, the estate owner was Erskine Owen Alleyne. He and his wife were not getting on well and his wife registered a Class F land charge – home rights against Erskine Alleyne with no reference to his middle name. Mr Alleyne then went to borrow money from a mortgage company and prior to lending him the money, they searched the Land Charges Register against the correct record of his name. That recorded in his purchase document Erskine Owen Alleyne. The effect was that because the mortgage company's search was correctly made, the defective registration was not binding on the mortgage company. So, registration of a land charge against the wrong name followed by a search against a correct name by the lender would mean that the equitable right that has been registered as a land charge is not binding.

Oak Cooperative Building Society v Blackburn [1967] CH 730

Case summary: What happens if registration is completed in the wrong name but the purchasers themselves searched against the wrong name? The owner was Francis David Blackburn, and this name was recorded in the purchase deed of the property and there was an estate contract registered against him, a Class C(iv) land charge. Unfortunately, in error it was recorded in the name Frank David Blackburn. Again, we have a situation where the owner Mr Blackburn went to borrow money from a mortgage company and prior to the lending the company made a search of the Land Charges Register but against the name Francis Davis Blackburn, so a further error. The Court of Appeal held the mortgage company were bound by the estate contract even though the contract had been registered against the wrong name.

Midland Bank v Green *[1981] AC 513*

Facts: A father owned a farm and granted his son an option to purchase the farm within 10 years for £22,500. There was then a family bust up and the father decided that he no longer wanted his son to become the owner of the farm. So, he sold his legal estate in the farm to his wife for £500 where the farm was worth £40,000. Now as we'll see, that option to purchase that the son was given should have given the son a right to buy the land if that was what he wanted to do and an option to purchase is a type of estate contract that can be registered as a Class C(iv) land charge. However, the son did not register it.

Held: The estate contract which has not been registered as a land charge is void against a purchaser of a legal estate who paid money (however small or large) under Section 4 of the LCA 1972. The wife was such as purchaser here. Therefore, the son could not enforce the contract against the wife.

Overreaching:
Birmingham Midshires Mortgage Services Ltd *v* Sabherwal *[2000] 80 P&CR 256*

Facts: Mrs Sabherwal lived in a house with her two sons and families. The sons were the legal owner who promised Mrs Sabherwal that she will always have a roof over her head in the house. The sons borrowed money by taking a mortgage from the *Birmingham Midshires Mortgage Services* (BMMS). The sons defaulted on the mortgage repayments. The issues were: (a) whether the nature of Mrs Sabherwal's interest in the house was a 'proprietary estoppel or constructive trust', and (b) whether any such interest is overreachable.

Held: The court held Mrs Sabherwal's interest in the house as a proprietary estoppel which has the same effect as a 'constructive trust'. Therefore, her right was overreachable for being an interest in a family home rather than in a commercial property.

Chapter 3: Registration of title (registered land)

The mirror principle and cracks in the mirror:
Strand Securities v Caswell *[1965]1 All ER 820*

Case summary: Caswell took a sub-lease of a flat and allowed his stepdaughter to live there free of rent. As a result, the stepdaughter was in occupation of the flat rather than Caswell. As he was not in occupation of the flat Caswell's sub-lease of the flat should have been registered by the Land Registry, but his actual occupation was not recognised through the occupation of the stepdaughter. The court held that the stepdaughter was not in actual occupation on Caswell's behalf because she was not acting as his agent.[1]

Facts: Caswell was a leaseholder of a flat in London for more than 21 years. No application was then made to register the sub-lease, or notice of it, at the Land Registry. In September 1961, the **first defendant**, who felt under a moral obligation to Mrs R., the second defendant, his stepdaughter, allowed her and her family to occupy the flat rent free and rates free, and thereafter they continued to occupy it. The first defendant owned a good deal of the furniture in the flat, occasionally used the flat, and had, it was assumed, a key to it.

On 21 March 1962, the registered lease was transferred to the plaintiffs, who knew of the sub-lease and of the occupation of the flat. The first defendant applied for registration of the sub-lease, the application stating that the land certificate for the registered lease was about to be deposited in the Land Registry on the transfer of the registered lease to the plaintiffs. **His application was received at the Land Registry on 5 April 1962**. It was the practice of the Land Registry to construe S. 64(1)*(a)* of the Land Registration Act, 1925, as requiring production of the lessor's land certificate on the first registration of a lease of registered land, and the registry accordingly refused to accept the first defendant's application until production of the land certificate of the registered lease. On 24 April 1962, the Land Registry received an application by the plaintiffs for registration of themselves as proprietors of the registered lease, accompanied by the land certificate. The registry treated the production of the land certificate as also serving the purposes of the first defendant's application and both applications as taking effect on the same day (April 24); the registry gave precedence to the plaintiffs' application (now head lease).

Issue: The plaintiff was seeking a declaration that the sub-lease of the first defendant is void for non-registration before the registration of the head lease.

CA held: The first defendant (Caswell) was **not in actual occupation** of the flat for the purposes of S. 70(1)*(g)* of the Land Registration Act, 1925, since the facts were that the first defendant allowed Mrs R to be in actual occupation of the flat on her own account, not as a caretaker or employee, and did not himself share occupation or receive a token rent.

Wishart v Credit and Mercantile [2015] EWCA Civ 655

Facts: The Appellant was a business partner of S. They both agreed that S would buy a house for the appellant from the profits of the business they both ran together. S bought the house but in the name of the company and then mortgage the house to a bank for a loan of £500,000. When S did not keep up repayments, the bank sold the

1 Although this case was decided under the LRA 1925, it is still a valid precedent on actual occupation.

house for £1.1m and it sought to keep £694,072.75 of the sale proceeds to realise its security. The appellant brought proceedings in which he claimed to be entitled to the full proceeds of sale as the beneficial owner of the property with an overriding interest, under Section 29 of and paragraph 2 of Schedule 3 to the Land Registration Act 2002, taking priority over the respondent's charge reason of his actual occupation of the property at the date when the charge was registered.

Held: The Court of Appeal (CA) held there are situations where a beneficial owner may lose his/her actual occupation as an overriding interest when s/he authorised an agent to act in a way that would enable the agent to deal with the property as an absolute owner. In this case, the CA adopted the 'Brocklesby principle' which prevents an occupier of a property from having an overriding interest against a legal owner.

Williams and Glyn's Bank Ltd v Boland *[1980] 2 ALL ER 408*

Facts: A husband and wife were equitable tenants in common of the matrimonial home by virtue of both having contributed to the purchase price, although only the husband's name appeared as the registered proprietor on the register in the Land Registry. The husband, without the wife's knowledge, mortgaged the home under a legal mortgage to a bank. Before lending, the bank did not inquire of the husband or the wife. The husband defaulted on the mortgage and the bank brought proceedings for, and were granted, possession. The issue was whether the wife had any interest in the property.

CA held: The wife was 'in actual occupation of the land', within S. 70(1)*(g)* of the Land Registration Act 1925, and accordingly had an 'overriding interest', within S. 70(1), which entitled her to remain in possession as against the bank and subject to which the bank had taken the mortgage. The bank appealed to the House of Lords, contending that the wife's beneficial interest in the house (i) was a minor interest under S. 3(xv)*(a)* of the Land Registration Act 1925 and (ii) was not capable of being overridden.

House of Lords (HL) held: What was needed is physical presence in the land. The word 'actual' was not intended to introduce any other qualifications but merely emphasised that what was needed was physical presence and not some entitlement in law. Since the wife was physically present in the matrimonial home, with all rights that occupiers had, including the right to exclude all others except those having similar rights, and the home was a matrimonial home intended to be occupied and in fact occupied by both spouses, both of whom had an interest in it, the wife was in actual occupation.

Even though the wife's interest, in so far as it existed under a trust for sale, was an equitable interest capable of being overreached and therefore a 'minor interest' within S. 3(xv) of the 1925 Act, it was also capable of being an overriding interest if it was protected by 'actual occupation', particularly if it was a house bought jointly by spouses to be lived in as a matrimonial home, because then it would be unreal to describe the spouses' interests as merely an interest in the proceeds of sale, or rents and profits until sale, and there was every reason why, in that event, such an interest should acquire the status of an overriding interest.

Per Curiam. (1) The fact that the overriding interest of a wife in actual occupation of a matrimonial home might also be capable of being protected by the registration of a **caution** is irrelevant.

In view of the widespread development of shared interests of ownership the departure from an easy-going practice of dispensing with inquiries as to occupation beyond that of the vendor and substitution of a practice of more careful inquiry extending to spouses and other members of the family, or even of persons outside it, cannot be considered unacceptable.

Link Lending Ltd. v Bustard [2010] EWCA Civ 424

Case summary: This case addresses the question about the scope of inspection required under Schedule 3 for buying an already registered land. The Court of Appeal held that temporary absence from occupation of the property does not invalidate actual occupation where the claimant was absent from her home for lengthy period while she was being looked after in a psychiatric unit. The court found **a degree of continuity and permanence** in the claimant's occupation based on a **clear intention to return**.

The insurance principle and indemnity by the Land Registry: Bakrania v Lloyds Bank *[2017] UK FTT (PC)*

Facts: The applicants were the former registered proprietors of a house that, they alleged, had been fraudulently transferred to joint proprietors of similar names. Those joint proprietors had then sold it to Mr and Mrs Souris, who now lived there. The Souris had bought it with the aid of a mortgage from Lloyds Bank, and the fraudsters and the money had disappeared. Consequently, the Bakranias applied for alteration of the register on the ground of mistake, asking that Mr and Mrs Souris and Lloyds Bank be removed from the register, with title reverting to them unencumbered (without any financial liability) by any mortgage.

Held: The Tribunal Judge decided that the Bakranias' 'right' to rectify did not have priority to the new proprietors. So, in the end, the Souris did take the title unencumbered and removing them would be a rectification against a proprietor in possession and would not succeed. However, Bakranias were allowed to receive indemnity.

The basic priority rule Halifax v Popeck *[2008] All ER 281*

Case analysis: The property concern in this case was a Bungalow which was bought by taking a mortgage (first mortgage) from Halifax which was not duly registered. The purchaser of the Bungalow took a second mortgage by fraud, but this was registered. The purchaser later defaulted to repay the second mortgage. Because the first mortgage from Halifax was an equitable mortgage for lack of registration the issue for the court was whether the second mortgagee was free from the first mortgage. The court held that Halifax's equitable mortgage should be preserved as a prior interest because the basic priority rule preserves any equitable interest under Ss. 28 and 29 of the LRA where a transfer of land had not been made 'for valuable consideration'. Since the second mortgage was carried out as part of a fraud, the general rule under S. 28 of the LRA 2002 applied. Thus, the transferee was held not to have given value (fraud) even though the transaction was a sale.

Gold Harp v Macleod *[2014] EWCA Civ 532*

Case analysis: The freeholder wanted to develop his property which was subject to a lease. As he could not otherwise evict the leaseholder, he applied to the Land Registry for removal of the lease based on false information. As a result of this, the lease was removed from the Registry by mistake. Once the lease was removed the freeholder granted a new lease to a company. However, the first leaseholder found out about his wrongful removal of the lease and made an application for rectification of the register by reinstating his lease. The second leaseholder opposed the application on the basis that the second lease would have priority had there been no mistake. The court held that the first leaseholder has priority under Schedule 4 paragraph 8 of the LRA 2002. It clarified that paragraph 8 enables the court or registrar not only to order restoration but also to decide on the priority. Thus, the court or registrar can change the special rule of priority (a purchaser has priority over all interests except those entered on the register and those overriding within Schedule 3) if doing that would give the party the priority which it should have had but for the mistake.

Chapter 4: Informal acquisition of title (implied trusts)

Resulting trusts

Lloyds Bank v Rosset *[1991] 1 AC 107*

Case analysis: The House of Lords stressed that the finding of an agreement or arrangement that the property is to be shared beneficially must be based on evidence of express discussions between the parties. In the absence of such evidence the courts would only infer a common intention where a person (who is not the legal owner) has made direct contributions to the purchase price, usually known as a resulting trust. In a resulting trust, the common intention is inferred to allocate a fair share according to the contribution of the co-owners.

Common Intention Constructive Trusts (CICT)

Oxley v Hiscock *[2004] EWCA Civ 546*

Case analysis: The Court of Appeal (CA) considered that where two persons contributed to the purchase of land conveyed into the name of one of them and where there was no agreement about the quantification of their respective shares, the court was entitled to take into account the whole course of conduct between the parties in determining what would be a fair share.

Lightfoot v *Lightfoot-Brown* [2005] EWCA Civ 201

Case analysis: the CA applied *Oxley* v *Hiscock*, holding that payment of money alone will not give rise to an equitable interest in the property. As made clear by Chadwick LJ in *Oxley*, there *must also be an agreement or understanding between the parties* that the payer should have such an interest. The need for communication was only held to be unnecessary in the *Oxley* case in respect to the size of the parties' beneficial interest.

Crossley v *Crossley* [2005] EWCA Civ 1581

Case analysis: *The CA distinguished oxley* [at paragraph 32]: Where the parties have reached a consensus on the beneficial interests in the property, the court will give effect to it, unless there is very good reason for not doing so, such as a subsequent renegotiation. The task of deciding the fair share having regard to the whole course of dealing in accordance with *Oxley* v *Hiscock*, need only be performed in the absence of an agreement, arrangement or understanding as to the nature and extent of the respective beneficial interests of the parties.

CICT – Joint name cases

Stack *v* Dowden *[2007] UKHL 17*

Facts: Ms Dowden and Mr Stack cohabited for 20 years and had 4 children. Their first home together was bought in 1983 for £30,000 in Ms Dowden's name, with a mortgage of £22,000 and a deposit of £8,000 from Ms Dowden's savings. That house was sold in 1993 and a new house was bought in joint names. £65,000 of the £190,000 purchase price was provided by a mortgage, and the remainder came from the proceeds of sale of the first house (£66,000 profit) and also from a bank account in Ms Dowden's name (£59,000). The relationship broke down in October 2002. After moving out of the house, Mr Stack obtained a court order under S. 14 TOLATA (Trust of Land and Appointment of Trustees Act, 1996) that he was entitled to half of the proceeds of sale of the house, now valued at £770,00, as a tenant in common, and obtained an order for sale.

Ms Dowden appealed and succeeded in proving that she was entitled to at least 65% of the proceeds of sale of the house. Stack appealed to HL, but he lost.

Held: The House of Lords held (leading judgment as given by Lady Hale) that, in the absence of a common intention the court will presume a joint tenancy in law and equity in joint name cases. However, this presumption is rebuttable by evidence of a common intention or change of a common intention in the course of time. The court will then infer the intention of the co-owners to decide a fair share between the parties.

The HL also observed that the burden is on the party looking to show that the parties intended their equitable interests to be different from their legal interests, and there are many relevant factors in deciding whether there was such a common intention. It would only be in unusual cases that a claimant would succeed in showing that the beneficial interests were different from the legal interests. *This was, however, just such an unusual case; since the parties had kept their finances separate even though they had cohabited for many years and had children together, this was strong evidence that they did not intend their shares to be equal even when the house was put into joint names*. Thus, the appeal was dismissed.

Jones v Kernott *[2011] UKSC 53*

Facts: This case concerns the correct approach to calculating beneficial interests in property where the legal title to the property is held in joint names by an unmarried couple but there is no express statement of how it is to be shared.

Ms Jones and Mr Kernott met in 1981. They had two children together. In 1985 they bought a house in Thundersley, Essex in their joint names. The price paid was £30,000 with a £6,000 deposit paid exclusively by the proceeds of sale from Ms Jones's previous home. No declaration was made as to how the beneficial interest in the property was to be held. The mortgage and upkeep of the house were shared between them. In 1986 they jointly took out a loan of £2000 to build an extension. Mr Kernott did some of the work himself. The relationship deteriorated and in 1993 Mr Kernott moved out. From that point onwards Ms Jones lived in the Thundersley property with both children. In 1996 Mr Kernott bought his own house in Benfleet, Essex. Over the years, the value of the Thundersley property increased and in 2006 Mr Kernott indicated that he wished to claim a beneficial share in it. In response, Ms Jones, in 2007, applied to the county court for a declaration under Section 14 of the Trusts of Land and Appointment of Trustees Act 1996 that she owned the entire beneficial interest in the property. By 2008 the property was valued at £245,000.

Held: The county court judge noted that the house was first bought to set up a family home. It was bought in joint names and a presumption arose that they intended to jointly share the beneficial ownership of it as well. However, since then their common intention had changed because Mr Kernott had ceased to make contributions towards the running of the house and had made only very limited contributions towards the support of their children. Moreover, it was mostly during that latter period that the value of the property had increased. The judge held that once the initial presumption of joint beneficial ownership is displaced and there is no further clear evidence as to the division of shares in the property it falls upon the court to infer or impute an intention to the parties as to the division of the property that they, as reasonable and fair people, would have intended. He decided that Mr Kernott was entitled to only a 10% share. Mr Kernott appealed to the High Court arguing that it was wrong for the court to infer or impute a change of common intention and further wrong for the judge, in effect, to substitute a division that he considered to be fair between the parties. The High Court judge dismissed his appeal. Mr Kernott appealed to the Court of Appeal which, by a majority, allowed his appeal. Ms Jones appealed to the Supreme Court which unanimously allowed the appeal and reinstated the order of the county court which is Mr Kernott to only have a 10% share.

CICT – Sole name case

Aspden v Elvy *[2012] EWHC 1387 (Ch)*

Facts: In 1986, the claimant (Mr Aspden) and defendant (Ms Elvy) moved into a property together (the farm). They began a relationship, and from around 1988 the defendant ran a cattery and kennels from the farm. The parties separated in late 1995 or early 1996. The defendant left the farm with the parties' two children and lived nearby but continued to run the cattery. In January 2006, the claimant transferred the ownership of a barn to the defendant (the barn). The barn covered most of the land on the farm. The claimant continued to live on the farm but occupied a static caravan. The parties took steps to convert the barn into a dwelling house. The conversion cost in total was around £90,000. A dispute arose as to the extent of the claimant's interest in the barn.

Issues: The principal issue was whether, and to what extent, the claimant had an interest in the barn. The defendant contended that she was the absolute owner of the barn, while the claimant contended that a constructive trust had been formed. It was common ground that the claimant had carried out labouring work at the property, but there was dispute as to whether that work had been for the benefit of the barn or for the claimant's caravan. It was also common ground that the claimant had made a financial contribution to the cost of the works. The claimant contended that his contribution had been in the region of £73,000, while the defendant contended that his contribution had been, in total, around £39,200. The defendant also contended that the claimant gave the money contributed as a gift to the defendant.

The court ruled: To succeed in proving an implied trust, the claimant needed to establish that the common intention of the parties had been that he should have an interest as a result of the physical and financial contributions he had made to the works. On the evidence, the claimant's account was to be preferred with reference to the amount of work that he had carried out on the barn and the extent of his financial contribution. It was impossible to conclude that the contributions, which were a substantial part of the claimant's assets, had been intended as gifts.

He had hoped and expected to live in the barn, and the defendant had been aware of that. The proper inference was that there had been a common intention that the claimant should have some interests in the barn because of his contributions. A fair assessment of the interest would be 25%, considering the value of the investment of the claimant's work and contributions, measured against the value of the barn at the time of trial. The court held that a declaration would be made to the effect that the barn was held by the claimant as to 25% for himself and the defendant as to 75% for herself.

Chapter 5: Co-ownership 2: Trusts of land

Williams v Hensman (1861) 70 E.R. 862

Case analysis: A money fund was bequeathed (by will) to be invested in stock to pay an annual payment (annuity) to A and on A's death the fund to go to her children. This case was about money not a land. However, the court outlined the principle of severance in this case. The court held that where joint tenants, by their conduct, treat their interests as severed, the effect of this, in severing the joint tenancy, is not prevented by the circumstance that they were not aware that their interests were originally joint.

Gore and Snell v Carpenter (1990) 60 P & CR 456, ChD

Facts: A husband and wife owned two properties as joint tenants. As their marital relationship had broken down, they decided to separate. They agreed in principle that their joint tenancy would end, and they would each have one of the houses as part of an overall separation agreement that they were conducting. The husband committed suicide before they reached a final agreement.

Issues: Whether the agreement in principle to sever the joint tenancy had in fact so severed it or whether more was needed to sever the joint tenancy.

Held: The joint tenancy had not been severed by the couple's agreement in principle. This is because the agreement was in preliminary form and was not finalised. Because of this, the joint tenancy had not been severed and the wife remained entitled to the right of survivorship.

Harris v Goddard [1983] 1 WLR 1203, CA

Case analysis: Mr and Mrs Harris bought a matrimonial home. Their relationship deteriorated. As a result, Mrs Harris filed a divorce petition where there was a prayer to transfer for or settlement or variation of settlement of the matrimonial home. Before the hearing, Mr Harris died in an accident. The issue was whether severance occurred. The court held that no severance occurred as the hearing was not completed so no judgment was delivered as to their shares in the matrimonial home.

Re K [1985] Ch 85

Case analysis: Husband left property to wife by will. Their relationship was worsening, and the wife was subject to domestic violence by the husband. One day, the husband attacked the wife, and the wife pointed a gun at him and asked to leave her alone. However, the wife accidentally killed the husband. She was charged with murder, but the court found her guilty of manslaughter. The husband's estate wished to rely on the provisions of the Forfeiture Act 1982 to ensure that the joint tenancy was severed, and the husband's beneficial interest vested in his estate. The issue was whether the wife would be forfeited of the will according to Section 2(2) of the Forfeiture Act 1982. The court held that considering the circumstances of the case – the hardship of the wife – she should be relieved from the application of the FA 1982. The court found that the unlawful killing of one beneficiary by another would sever the joint tenancy under the FA 1982 as occurred in this case, but the court should exercise its discretion here to prevent hardship.

Begum v Hafiz [2015] EWCA Civ 801

Facts: The parties bought a residential property for the each of them in equal shares. The mother (claimant) and her two sons (defendants) were the parties. Due to a dispute between the parties the mother issued proceedings to seek an order requiring the second defendant (one of the sons) to sell his share in the property to the first defendant (another son).

Issues: At a trial of a preliminary issue, the judge held that she had no jurisdiction to make such an order. However, she considered that, by virtue of the discretionary power conferred on her by Ss. 14 and 15 of the Trusts of Land and Appointment of Trustees Act 1996, she had jurisdiction to make an order directing that the property be sold. The first defendant was to have the opportunity to purchase it at a price to be determined by the court and, if he did not do so within six weeks of the determination of the price, the property was to be sold on the open market with liberty for each of the parties to bid for it.

The second defendant appealed. The claimant and first-defendant cross-appealed by way of respondent's notice.

The second defendant submitted that the judge had had no jurisdiction to make such an order and, even if she had, then it had not been a proper exercise of her jurisdiction under the Act. The claimant and first defendant submitted that the judge had had the jurisdiction to make the order originally sought, namely, the purchase by the first defendant of the second defendant's beneficial interest in the property.

Held: The appeal would be dismissed. The cross-appeal would be dismissed.

The court did not have power under S. 14 of the Act to order or direct that one beneficiary under a trust of land sell or transfer their beneficial interest to another beneficiary. The clear object and effect of Ss. 14 and 15 was to confer upon the court a wider discretion, exercised upon the basis of wider considerations, than what might be enjoyed by the trustees themselves, acting without either the consent of their beneficiaries or an order of the court. Section 15(1) (a) might bring into play the intention of the person who created the trust that benefits be conferred upon beneficiaries. All that departed from the general rule of equity which required the trustees single-mindedly to advance the interests of the beneficiaries as a class, without preferring some of them over others. None of that meant that the court would act unfairly, unjustly, or capriciously as between beneficiaries in giving directions to trustees under S. 14(2). It simply showed that, in exercising its powers in circumstances where, necessarily, the beneficiaries were in dispute with each other about what should be done with the trust property, the court was not rigidly constrained by those rules of equity which might, pursuant to S. 6(6) of the Act, constrain the trustees themselves.

Chapter 6: Landlord and tenant (the law of leases)

Strand Securities v Caswell [1965] Ch. 958

Case analysis: A tenant of a flat allowed his stepdaughter to live there rent-free. Since she was a bare licensee of the flat, she had no right that could constitute an overriding interest, even though she was in actual occupation. [Discussed in detail above under Chapter 3 cases.]

Street v Mountford (1985) AC 809

Case analysis: Street granted a licence to Mountford to occupy two rooms at a weekly rent. The agreement included clauses which required 14 days' notice for termination by either party. The agreement was titled as a 'licence agreement'. The issue was whether the agreement was a tenancy despite being labelled as a licence agreement. The court held that the agreement was a lease. The court recognised that labelling an agreement is not conclusive but the actual nature of the obligations under the agreement. As Mountford had unrestricted access to the rooms he had exclusive possession and hence was a tenant. The court also held that Mountford was entitled to protection as tenant under Rents Act for his right to a fair rent.

Antoniades v Villiers (1990) 1 AC 417

Case analysis: An unmarried couple signed separate agreements for the occupation of a single bedroom flat. These agreements gave the landowner certain rights that were unlikely to be exercised in practice such as the right to nominate another occupier. The court held that this was an attempt by the landowner to avoid the grant of a tenancy by artificially destroying the tenants' proprietary right.

Bruton v London & Quadrant Housing Trust (1999) UKHL 26

Case analysis: The Housing Trust allocated council property to Bruton as a tenant. This created a lease, but the Housing trust could not assign a lease because they were neither a freeholder nor a head-leaseholder of those properties. It was the council who was able to assign a lease. As a result, there was no lease between Bruton and the Housing Trust by law. In this situation, Bruton asked the Housing Trust to repair the property, but the latter sent a notice that asked the former to vacate the property. The issue was whether Bruton was a tenant or mere licensee. The court considered the issue that the Housing Trust cannot create a tenancy in law but if the court did not recognise a tenancy Bruton would not have any remedy. As a result, the House of Lords recognised a non-proprietary lease in favour of Bruton.

Comments: This case is an example of a deviation from '*namo dat quod non habet*' principle, i.e., one cannot assign or create an interest which s/he himself/herself does not have. So, this case is an exceptional one and hence is not the most reliable authority in this area of law. Therefore, every case should be decided on its own merit.

Berrisford v Mexfield (2011) UKSC 52

Facts: Ms Berrisford entered into an occupancy agreement with Mexfield where she agreed to pay rent weekly. The only express provisions of the occupancy agreement dealing with its termination provided that it could be determined, under clause 5, by Ms Berrisford giving Mexfield one month's notice in writing and, under clause 6, by Mexfield 'by the exercise of the right of re-entry specified in this clause but ONLY in [certain specified] circumstances' which did not include the giving of notice to quit. Because Mexfield was a mutual housing association the only statutory protection from which Ms Berrisford benefited was a right to (a) not be evicted without a court order and (b) at least four weeks' notice to quit. Ms Berrisford remained in occupation and complied with her obligations under the occupancy agreement until (apparently through no fault of her own) she fell into arrears with her rent, which she soon paid off. Rather than invoking any of the provisions of clause 6 of the agreement, Mexfield sought to end Ms Berrisford's occupancy by serving a notice to quit.

Issue: There were two issues:

(a) Whether the occupancy agreement was a tenancy because it was of uncertain duration.
(b) Whether the occupancy agreement was an implied periodic tenancy.

Held: The Supreme Court held that if the uncertain term was granted to an individual (but not to a company) then the agreement could be treated as a 'lease for life'. The court applied Section 149(6) LPA 1925 which provides that a 'lease for life' granted at a rent or for a premium are converted to a lease for 90 years, terminable by death (if earlier).

Comments: As a result, a lease for an uncertain term can be saved under this case. However, it is important for you to note that this is an exceptional case, and the court may reject or restrict its application in cases where there is no valid consent between the parties. See *Southward Housing Co-operative v. Walker* [2015] EWHC 1615 (Ch).

Chapter 7: Licences and proprietary estoppel

Wilmott v Barber (1880) 15 ChD 96

Case analysis: The defendant, Barber, took a lease (head lease) from a landowner. He then granted a sub-lease to the claimant, Wilmot, with a promise that the latter would be able to buy the head lease. Relying on this promise the claimant laid out a foundation to build a timber yard. The court held that the claimant, Wilmot, could not invoke proprietary estoppel because the landowner (the lessor of the head lease) did not know about the promise made by the defendant. As a result, the fifth criterion was not satisfied, i.e., the owner of the land over which the right is claimed must know of the existence of their own rights, and that these are inconsistent with the alleged rights of the claimant.

Taylor Fashions v Liverpool Victoria Trustees (1982) QB 133

Case analysis: Liverpool Victoria Trustees, the defendant, granted a lease to Taylor Fashions (the claimant) with an option for the latter to renew the lease. Although the defendant believed that the lease was renewable by the claimant, they argued that this option was not enforceable. The claimant made a PE claim based on defendant's action that encouraged the claimant to improve the leasehold property, so this was a promise made by the claimant. The court held that the defendant had encouraged the claimant to make improvements, so their conduct satisfy the four criteria for PE, i.e., representation, reliance, detriment, and unconscionable.

Hoyl Group Ltd v Cromer Town Council (2015) EWCA Civ 782

Facts: Hoyl Group, the claimant, was granted a tenancy of a basement flat by the defendant Cromer Town Council. The flat was initially accessible via an internal door but later the claimant obtained permission to access the flat over the garden and stop up the internal door. The council not only approved the plan but also encouraged the alteration of the layout of the flat and the provision for the external access to the flat.

Issue: Whether knowledge by the landowner of the claimant's belief (albeit mistaken) is necessary to uphold a PE.

Held: The court held that knowledge by the landowner is not always necessary to satisfy a claim of PE. In this case, the active encouragement by the council (landowner) was sufficient.

Thorner v Major (2009) 1 WLR 776

Facts: The claimant worked on the defendant's farm for more than a decade without any payment. The defendant was under the belief that he would inherit the farm once the defendant died. Although the defendant once paid a bonus to the claimant, he never explicitly told that the claimant would inherit the farm. However, the defendant initially made a will where he left the farm to the claimant, but he retracted the will before his death.

Issue: Whether PE can arise in the absence of an explicit promise.

Held: The House of Lords decided that explicit promise is not always necessary. It is sufficient if the conduct of the defendant conveys a message that a reasonable claimant would belief that they would have a proprietary interest in the land.

Cobbe v Yeoman's Row Management [2008] UKHL 55

Facts: This dispute was in relation to a land between a developer (Cobbe) and a landowner (Yeoman). The landowner orally agreed with Cobbe that he would sell the land at an agreed upfront price once Cobbe obtains a planning permission to build flats on the land. Cobbe agreed to bear all the expenditure for obtaining the planning permission. Once the permission was obtained, Yeoman asked for a higher price. As the agreement was not in writing, it did not follow Section 2 of the LP(MP) Act 1989. In this situation, Cobbe claimed a proprietary estoppel in the property.

Issue: The issue was whether an orally made agreement, which did not materialise in writing, can be saved by invoking PE.

Held: The House of Lords held that the requirement of an agreement to be in writing cannot be invoked by the back door by claiming PE. This is a sale agreement with respect to a property which the parties agreed to buy and sell respectively once the planning permission was obtained. Although there is evidence of unconscionability by Yeoman, this was not enough to invoke PE.

Comments: Please note that, although the House of Lords refused to recognise an estoppel it recognised the unjust enrichment of the landowner (Yeoman) which was made because of obtaining the planning permission. As a result, the court ordered Yeoman to compensate Cobbe for his service in obtaining the planning permission.

Creasy v Sole [2013] EWHC 1410

Case analysis: The defendants were the administrators of the deceased parents of the claimants. The parents owned property in joint tenancy and tenancy in common. They also left separate wills to leave their property (including those held in joint tenancy). The claimants' claim was based proprietary estoppel where they claimed that the deceased promised them to own their respective land which the claimant occupied to farm. However, there was no evidence except the account of the claimants that such promises were made. The court held that in the absence of corroboration the claimant's account only is insufficient to uphold a claim for proprietary estoppel.

Greasley v Cooke [1980] 3 All ER 710

Case analysis: A young woman, Greasley, started to work as a maid in a house where she entered into a relationship with the claimant's father. Since then, she was not paid for her work for the family, but she was assured by the claimant's father that she could live in the house for life. After the man died, the claimant brought a proceeding to evict her. She claimed proprietary estoppel. The Court of Appeal held that where there is evidence of a promise made and a detrimental reliance suffered, it is permissible for the court to assume that reliance has occurred.

Orgee v Orgee [1997] EGCS 152

Case analysis: The defendant orally agreed to farm the claimant's land based on a promise made by the claimant that the former would be granted a tenancy. The parties did not agree on a tenancy. As a result, the claimant brought a claim for possession against the defendant. In response, the defendant claimed proprietary estoppel. The court decided that the defendant cannot successfully claim a PE because their belief was not sufficiently concrete. It concluded that, in this case, the defendant would have suffered the detriment anyway, even if the claimant had not made any promises.

Lloyd v Dugdale [2001] EWCA Civ 1754

Case analysis: The defendant decided for his company to start building work on the claimant's land. In exchange of these arrangements, the claimant made a promise that he would grant a sub-lease to the defendant. The promise was made according to the assurance given by the landowner. The claimant refused to grant the sub-lease and brought a possession proceeding against the defendant. The defendant claimed proprietary estoppel. The court held that the defendant cannot claim PE because the promise was not made to him, nor that he suffered any detriment. Rather, the promise was made to the company which had a separate entity from that of the defendant.

Gillett v Holt [2001] Ch 210

Case analysis: The defendant, Holt, made a promise to the claimant, Gillett, that if the latter left the college and worked in the former's farm then he would own it at the defendant's death. Based on the promise, the claimant started to work on the farm. Subsequently, their relationship became worse, and the defendant made a will to leave the farm to somebody else. The claimant made a claim for PE. The court held that the claimant's claim for PE was lawful because Gillett suffered a detriment by giving up college. So, a detriment is not confined to money only. The court also held that unconscionability exists even when the assurance is withdrawn after detrimental reliance.

Matchmove v Dowding [2016] EWCA Civ 1233

Case analysis: Two friends agreed to buy and sell a land and a meadow. Although the sale of the land was completed, the sale of the meadow was delayed due to a dispute about an easement with the neighbour. The purchaser contributed to the funding of the dispute. After winning the dispute, the seller only wanted to sell half of the meadow. The court held that a common intention constructive trusts arose between the friends because there was an express agreement between them, detrimental reliance by the purchaser, and it would be unconscionable for the defendant to deny the claimant's ownership in the meadow which was agreed between the parties.

Comments: This case is an example where the court is likely to enforce an unwritten agreement as a CT rather than PE. This is because in a CT claim a common intention can be discerned from the conduct of the parties where they entered into a verbal agreement, but such agreement is not necessary to uphold a PE claim.

Chapter 8: Easements and *profits á prendre*

Re Ellenborough Park (1956) Ch 131

Case analysis: People who owned houses around a park were granted the right to use it as a 'leisure garden', but during the Second World War it was taken over by the government. If the house owners had been deprived of a legal right, then they were entitled to compensation under a statute. The only possible legal right was an easement on the facts. Eventually, the house owners succeeded in convincing the Court of Appeal that the right to use the park was an easement. Four factors were held to be relevant to decide whether an easement exists. Namely, a) there must be a dominant and a servient tenement; (b) the easement must accommodate the dominant tenement; (c) the dominant and servient tenements must be owned or occupied by different persons; and (d) the easement must be capable of forming the subject-matter of a grant.

Hill v Tupper (1863) 2 H & C 121

Case analysis: The owner of a canal granted the claimant a right to put pleasure boats on the canal. The issue was whether this right was an easement. It was held that this right was not an easement because this was not sufficiently connected to the claimant's land. The right to put pleasure boats on the canal was a more personal right which benefited the claimant personally.

Comments: Please note that an easement can be granted where it would confer a commercial benefit to the dominant land. However, this case is an example where a mere personal right cannot be an easement.

Wheeldon v Burrows [1879] 12 (Ch) D 31

Case analysis: Wheeldon owned a workshop and an adjacent land which he put up for sale. Both the land and workshop were sold separately to different purchasers. The purchaser of the workshop (Burrows) claimed a right to light as an easement because the workshop could only have light through the small windows that it had in the wall next to the adjacent land which the new purchaser of the land blocked out. The court held that, in a grant of land, there may be implied in favour of the grantee those rights in the nature of easements which are continuous and apparent, and necessary to the reasonable enjoyment of the property granted, and which have been, and are at the time of the grant, used by the grantor for the benefit of the part granted.

Comments: This is a leading case that created a *quasi-easement* situation in common law where an apparent and necessary easement can be held as an implied grant.

Wright v Macadam [1949] 2 KB 744

Case analysis: The landlord (defendant) agreed to lease a flat to the claimant with a permission for the latter to store coal in a coal-shed located in the garden of the building. The lease was then renewed but the landlord asked for money for using the shed as the new tenancy agreement did not stipulate anything about the use of the shed. The court held that the defendant cannot ask for money because the use of the shed was an easement under Section 62, LPA 1925.

Chapter 9: Freehold covenants

Tulk v Moxhay [1848] 41 ER 1143

Facts: Tulk sold a property in Leicester Square to a purchaser who promised that he would not build on the property so the structure of the Leicester Square would remain unchanged. The purchaser then sold the property to another person followed by other multiple sales and eventually bought by the defendant (Moxhay) who wanted to build on the property. He argued that he was not the original covenantor so he can build.

Issue: Whether the covenant can run with the land to find a future owner who was not the original covenantor.

Held: It was held that *the original parties intended to run the covenant with the land* as all purchasers were informed about this so Moxhay was bound by this.

Rhone v Stephens [1994] 2 AC 310

Facts: The claimant (Rhone) bought a cottage which shared the same room with a house. The original covenantor, the owner of the house, promised that he would keep the room of the cottage in a good condition. The house was transferred by the original covenantor and now is owned by the defendant (Stephens). The cottage room started leaking. The claimant brought a claim to enforce the covenant against the defendant who argued that the burden of a positive covenant did not run with the land.

Issue: Whether the burden of a positive covenant runs with a freehold land.

Held: The burden of a positive covenant does not run with the land under Section 79 LPA 1925.

Swift Investments v Combined English Stores [1989] AC 632

Case analysis: This case had decided the principle that 'in order to be enforceable a covenant must touch and concern the land'. The defendant covenanted that they would be responsible to pay any outstanding rent of the property if the sub-tenant fails. The subtenant defaulted and the defendant refused to pay. As a result of this, the claimant applied to the court to recover the sum owed. The court held that the claimant could recover the sum owned as it was touching and concerned the land.

Halsall v Brizell [1957] Ch 169

Case analysis: In a scheme of development the purchasers were given the benefit of using various roads with a covenant that they would need to maintain those. The covenant also provided that each plot in the scheme would be subject to the burden of this positive covenant. Subsequently, one of the plots was sold and converted into three flats. The new owner of the plot claimed that he was only liable to contribute the expense for one plot only but not each of the three flats. The court held that since the purchaser enjoyed the benefit of using the roads, they must fulfil their obligation to pay towards the maintenance costs for each of the flats under the principle of mutual burden and benefit. The court recognised the principle and stated that 'a man cannot take benefit under a deed without subscribing to the associated obligations'.

Elliston v Reacher [1908] 2 Ch 374

Case analysis: This case concerned enforcement of a restrictive/negative covenant against successors in title in a building scheme. The building society sold plots to purchasers who agreed that they would not run a hotel, tavern, pub, or manufacturing plant in their plots. Subsequently, one of the plots was sold to a purchaser who started a hotel business in the property. The court recognised the validity of the covenant in a building scheme subject to the satisfaction of the following conditions:

- All purchasers acquire their property from the same vendor.
- The vendor has divided the estate into plots prior to the sales.
- The vendor intended the restrictive covenants to continue for the benefit of all the plots.
- Every purchaser must acquire the plot on the understanding that the covenants benefit all the other plots in the scheme.

Chapter 10: Adverse possession

Pye v Graham [2002] 3 WLR 221

Facts: Pye sold his farmhouse in 1977 where he agreed that the new buyer would be able to graze in the land held by the former (the disputed land). The Grahams bought the farmhouse in 1982. In 1983, they entered into a grazing agreement with Pye where they agreed to pay £2,000 annually for grazing in the disputed land. When the Grahams asked to renew the agreement, Pye rejected as he wished to apply for planning permission to build on the disputed land. Pye also asked the Grahams to vacate the land. However, the Grahams did not do that but continued to graze on the land. They also put a padlock on the gate of the disputed land which was enclosed by hedges. In 1999, Pye issued proceedings against the Grahams to recover possession of the land.

Issue: Whether the Grahams have a defence as adverse possessors.

Held: The Court held that the Grahams had a valid defence as adverse possessors of the land. They had the intention to possess the land as adverse possessors and also were in factual possession of the land. The evidence to have a padlock on the gate of the disputed enclosed land by the Grahams showed their factual possession and exclusive physical control of the land.

Baxter v Mannion [2011] 1 WLR 1594

Case analysis: The adverse possessor managed to become a registered proprietor because the application to register him was not objected. However, after the registration it transpired that the adverse possessor did not actually complete the required ten years of adverse possession. As a result, the claimant applied to rectify the register based on the mistake the led to the registration. The claimant was successful because, although the rules of registration were applied correctly, there was a mistake due to not completing the required period of ten years' adverse possession.

Zarb v Parry [2011] EWCA Civ 1306

Facts: Zarb and Parry were neighbours. They both bought property from different sellers and the plan attached to the transfer showed that the boundary between the properties ran to the north of a hedge which was on Zarb's land. Parry erected a fence further south of the hedge (the disputed strip of land) which Zarb tried to interrupt by planting stakes. The court at first instance held that Parry had acquired title by adverse possession of a strip of land between the boundary and the hedge which formed part of their garden. Zarb appealed against a decision.

Held: The Court of Appeal held that, the court of first instance was correct to hold that Parry had successfully completed ten years of adverse possession of the strip of disputed land. It found that although it was clear that Zarb intended that they should recover possession, but they did not retake possession in any meaningful sense.

Malik v Fassenfelt [2013] EWCA Civ 798

Facts: Mr Malik bought a plot near the Heathrow airport in London in 2003. Malik's predecessor used the land as a market garden centre which was closed down when Mr Malik purchased the plot. Mr Malik applied for a planning permission to build office spaces on the plot, but this was refused. Eventually, the plot became a dumping ground for cars and fly tipping. A group of trespassers recovered the plot and converted the dumping ground into its earlier feature, i.e., a market garden centre, and began to live there. Mr Malik issued proceedings to evict the trespassers who raised a defence under Article 8 ECHR (private and family life).

Issue: Whether an Article 8 defence can be legally made against a claim for possession by a private landowner against the trespassers.

Held: The Court of Appeal held that, Article 8 could apply where squatters had trespassed onto private land and set up a home there, but it would be rare for their removal to be so disproportional to be contrary to the Article.

Best v Chief Land Registrar [2015] EWCA Civ 17

Case analysis: In this case, the Land Registry's original view that 'if the applicant based his or her possession facts which would amount to a criminal offence then the application for title by adverse possession had to be rejected outright', was challenged in an appeal to the Court of Appeal (CA). Best's application was rejected by the Land Registry on this ground, but his appeal was successful in the CA. The court held that the commission of the criminal offence (such as trespass) was not itself a bar to achieving title by adverse possession.

Chapter 11: Mortgages

Santley v *Wilde* [1899] 2 Ch 474

Case analysis: The claimant was a leaseholder of a theatre. To run the theatre, he took a mortgage from a bank secured against the lease. The mortgage deed required the claimant to pay not only the money borrowed but one-third of the net profits to the lender until the end of the mortgage term, i.e., five years. The claimant argued that the provision to pay the net profits is a barrier to the equity of redemption (mortgagor's right to redeem the mortgage even after the default). The court considered the nature of the theatre business and held that there was no barrier to the equity of redemption. This is because the mortgagee invested money in a risky project, i.e., theatre, which could suffer loss and in which case the bank would lose the money it lent. Therefore, the provision to pay one-third of the net profits was not unconscionable or oppressive.

Alliance & Leicester v Slayford [2001] 3 HLR 743

Case analysis: The Court of Appeal recognised the lender's right to sue the borrower under the mortgage contract where the borrower accepted a contractual obligation to make repayments. The court held that this is not an abuse of the process by the lender to sue the borrower under the contract particularly where the former cannot obtain a possession order because a third party has an equitable interest in the mortgaged property, i.e., when the wife has an equitable interest.

Swift 1st v Chief Land Registrar (2015) Ch 602

Case analysis: A fraudster forged the signature of a registered proprietor of a property to execute a mortgage in favour of Swift 1st. After the fraud was found Swift agreed with the Land Registrar that the register should be rectified. The register was rectified to remove the charge. However, Swift claimed for indemnity. The Chief Registrar argued that Swift did not suffer any losses by the rectification because the charge was never enforceable against the real owner of the property charged. The court held that registration guaranteed the charge even though this was registered due to a mistake that resulted from the fraud. Therefore, Swift is entitled to an indemnity. The court also held that the statuary right to rectification can subsist as an overriding interest where the real owner still is in actual occupation.

United Bank of Kuwait v Sahib [1997] Ch 107

Case analysis: The defendant, Sahib, was a co-owner of the mortgaged property. He held the title deeds of that property on behalf the lender. As a result, an equitable mortgage was created between the co-owners and the lender. However, the United Bank of Kuwait (the claimant) had a legal mortgage executed by deed. As a result of this, the claimant argued that the legal mortgage takes priority over the equitable one because the latter was not completed in writing. The court concluded that a mortgage which has not been concluded by a deed or enforceable written contract is void.

Kinane v Alimamy Mackie-Conteh [2005] EWCA Civ 45

Case analysis: In this case the claimant (Kinane) relied on an oral agreement where the defendant (Alimamy) agreed to charge a property to the claimant. The agreement was void due to not being in writing. However, the claimant argued that the agreement was enforceable as proprietary estoppel. The court upheld the claimant's argument. This was an exceptional case where the court awarded proprietary estoppel to give effect an unwritten mortgage agreement to avoid unconscionablity to the claimant.

Royal Bank of Scotland v Etridge (No.2) [2001] 4 All ER 449

Case analysis: This case is concerned with several appeals where homeowners had mortgaged their properties to secure loans by the husbands to fund their businesses. The wives claimed that they signed the mortgage deed under an undue influence from their husbands. The House of Lords held that in this situation a solicitor must ensure that the parties signed the mortgage deed with free consent. This is particularly the case where there is conflict of interests, i.e., where one of the parties is going to be benefited from the loan.

Rooks Rider v J.R. Steel [1993] 4 All ER 716

Facts: The plaintiff solicitors acted for H Inc, a Louisiana corporation which had agreed to lend £35m to C Ltd at interest of 10% per annum, on condition that C Ltd would in advance provide H Inc with a letter of credit to cover the first year's interest and would pay H Inc's costs. The plaintiffs were asked to prepare the loan contract as a matter of urgency. They agreed to act upon a written undertaking being given by the defendants, C Ltd's solicitors, 'to pay your proper fees and disbursements in connection with the preparation and execution of the proposed Loan Agreement between your Client ... and our Client ... whether the matter proceeds to completion or not'. It later transpired that H Inc had no funds and its directors never intended to make the loan but intended to use the loan agreement as a means of fraudulently securing money from C Ltd or elsewhere in advance of the loan. The plaintiffs nevertheless sought to enforce the undertaking given by the defendants in respect of the plaintiffs' costs of preparing the loan documentation amounting to £31,918. They applied for an order to that effect, pursuant to the court's inherent jurisdiction in relation to solicitors' conduct. The defendants contended that they were entitled to refuse to pay because the undertaking had been vitiated by H Inc's fraudulent intention.

Held: It was professional misconduct for a solicitor, without lawful justification, not to follow an undertaking. On the facts, the plaintiffs were not affected by any illegality from the fraudulent intention to H Inc in entering into the transaction, and there was therefore no lawful justification for the defendants not to comply with the undertaking, since the plaintiffs had no notice of any illegality and were in no sense successors in title of persons affected by the illegality as they had insisted on the undertaking for their own protection. The defendants would therefore be directed to follow their undertaking.

First Plus Financial Group plc v Hewett [2010] EWCA Civ 312

Facts: Wife persuaded by husband to agree to re-mortgage matrimonial home to refinance husband's debts. Husband having clandestine affair and later obtaining divorce.

Issue: Was the affair a material fact that should have been disclosed to the wife?

Held: The Court of Appeal held that, for an obligation of candour and fairness to be owed by the husband, it was necessary to show that the wife reposed trust and confidence in him. Usually that meant trust and confidence in the conduct of the family's affairs. The court found that it would be wrong to confine a husband's obligation of candour and fairness when proposing a risky financial transaction to his wife as confined to cases where the wife meekly followed her husband's directions without question. The purpose of an obligation of candour was that the wife should be able to make an informed decision properly and fairly appraised of the relevant circumstances. In the instant case, the husband's concealment of his affair from the defendant had amounted to the exercise of undue influence against her, sufficient to vitiate the re-mortgage transaction as between them. The defendant had reposed a sufficient degree of trust and confidence in the husband to give rise to an obligation of candour and fairness owed to her.

Comments: As a solicitor, you must disclose any clandestine affair of one of your clients to another, particularly where a married or unmarried couple instructs you, and you found out that one of them was having a clandestine affair. This is to avoid any conflict of interest between the clients and prevent a financial transaction from taking effect because of potential misrepresentation or fraud.

Appendix B
Problem questions

Chapter 1: Preliminary information before you start studying Land law for SQE1

Helen owns a house, registered land, which she rented out to Lauren. They signed a contract of a lease for six months fixed term followed by a monthly tenancy. Lauren moved in immediately. One month later, Lauren found out that one of her childhood friends, Niamh, was homeless. Lauren invited her to move into the spare room until she could find somewhere else to live. Two months later, Helen executed a deed to sell off the house to Tom. Tom's proprietorship was registered immediately at the Land Registry. Tom was aware of the lease agreement between Helen and Lauren.

Three months later, Lauren fell out with Niamh, so she wanted her to leave immediately. Can Lauren ask her to leave? When Tom found out that Lauren asked Niamh to leave the property, he became very unhappy about this. He asked Lauren to vacate the house within a week. Can Tom do that?

Answer: See the companion website.

Chapter 2: Unregistered Land law

David and Suzie were in a relationship and studying for a degree in business studies. In July 2012, David and Suzie completed their degree and started working in their first jobs. They were living with their parents until November 2014 when David offered Suzie to come and live with him in his house. David purchased this house in September 2014 for £200,000. He paid £20,000 as a deposit and raised the rest of the money (£180,000) by way of securing a legal mortgage.

Suzie moved into David's house, which is an unregistered land, in November 2014. Since then, she had been paying the utility bills and monthly shopping expenses. David was solely responsible for the repayments of mortgage. In December 2016, Suzie gave birth to their first child Megan. They had another child in January 2018 whose name is Charlotte. Within ten days of Charlotte's birth, David won a lottery and paid off the outstanding mortgage payment. He then became a heavy gambler and spent all of his savings, including the money that he won in the lottery.

DOI: 10.4324/9781003204954-13

In the beginning of 2019, David lost his job and as a result suffered from serious financial problems. He wanted to start a new business but was not financially able to do so. He applied for a bank loan but due to his unemployed status, he did not succeed. His relationship with Suzie had suffered due to his irresponsible gambling.

In June 2020, David booked an appointment with a local estate agent, Nicholas Estates, to sell his house. Nicholas Estates appointed Peter, a surveyor, to conduct a comprehensive survey and prepare a valuation report on David's house. Whilst conducting the survey, Peter saw a room where a wardrobe was full of women's clothing, shoes, and accessories. When Peter asked about this, David told him that he had split up with Suzie a few months ago and she had moved out already. He also told him that Suzie would be coming to take her personal belongings very soon. Peter produced a valuation report of the property where he valued it for £350,000 and there was nothing stated in the report about the existence of personal belongings of Suzie. Nicholas Estates advertised the house in the market for sale. They had also arranged viewings with a few potential buyers. In November 2020, Chris made an offer to purchase David's house for £350,000 which the latter accepted. David and Chris had completed a contract of sale on 30 November 2020 where they agreed to complete the sale by the end of January 2021. Chris did not register the contract.

Due to unprecedented financial difficulties, David was involved heavily in gambling. This had resulted in the worsening of the relationship between David and Suzie. In August 2021, David changed his mind and decided to mortgage his property in order to get some money so that he can start a new business and do some gambling. He discussed this with Nicholas Estates who acted also as a mortgage broker for David. Nichols Estates approached AB Bank plc for a mortgage on behalf of David and produced the valuation report completed by Peter. Based on the valuation report, AB Bank plc issued a loan of £200,000 in exchange for a mortgage deed of David's house.

David started a new restaurant in the town centre. However, the business was not going very well and as a result, he failed to keep up the repayments of the mortgage. January 2022 has now passed. On the one hand, Chris has asked David to complete the sale according to the contract entered into on 30 November 2020, and AB Bank plc has sent a legal notice to David to vacate the property on the other.

Advise Suzie, Chris, and AB Bank plc on their legal position in relation to David's house.

Answer: See the companion website.

Chapter 3: Registration of title

1. Jemina is the owner of 'Wren cottage' which is a registered property with the HM Land Registry. In March 2020, she let her father Mohammad to stay in a spare room of the cottage. She said to her father that you can live in the spare room as a nationwide

lockdown is going to start soon, so you may find it difficult to find another accommodation, but the room is in a poor condition, so you would need to spend some money to fix the wall, heating system, and electric connections. Mohammad spent about £10,000 on the spare room to carry out the repairs. In January 2021, Jemina lost her job so she mortgaged the cottage with a bank so she could run a small business. Due to the COVID-19 pandemic, her business was not going very well and as a result she could not keep up the mortgage repayments. The bank gave her a payment holiday of about six months, but she still could not make any repayments. She asked Mohammad but he could not offer any help except paying the bills. In January 2022, the bank sent notice to Jemina notifying their intention to sell the cottage to recover the mortgage debt. The cottage was sold to James in March 2022 who checked the register and found only Jemina as the registered owner of the cottage. He personally inspected the property and the spare room where Mohammad was living but never questioned this. James now has found out that Mohammad is unwilling to vacate the property unless he receives the money that he spent to renovate the property, pay the bills, and until he finds an alternative accommodation.

Advise James.

Answer: See the companion website.

2. Umar is the registered proprietor of Rose Cottage. He bought this property in 2013 where the purchase price came from a gift from his parents. Recently, Umar has been offered a place at the university which is located in another part of the country. As a result, he stays in a privately rented flat during most of the weekdays but comes back to Rose Cottage during the weekends. In early 2022, a fraudster produced fake ID documents to a conveyancer impersonating Umar and sold the cottage to Jemina who knew nothing about the fraud. As a result, Jemina became the registered proprietor. Once Umar became aware of the registration of Jemina as the owner of the cottage, he made inquiries and found out that he had been a victim of fraud. He contacted Jemina to let her know about the fraud. Since then, Jemina has been trying to find the fraudster but without any success so far. The fraudster has disappeared with the money.

Advise Jemina and Umar.

Answer: See the companion website.

Chapter 4: Co-ownership 1: Informal acquisition of title (implied trusts)

Brian is a successful businessperson, and Sarah is an accountant. They met in 2009 at an investment banking conference. In 2010, Brian and Sarah bought a flat to live together as an unmarried couple. They each contributed half of the deposit for the purchase of the flat but the title to the property and the mortgage were registered in Brian's name. Brian made regular payments towards the mortgage. Sarah paid all the household bills. They both shared the cooking, cleaning, and expenses for household repairs.

In 2015, Brian and Sarah had their first child, Charlotte. In 2017, they had another child, Kane. Since the birth of their second child, they needed a larger accommodation. In 2018, they sold the flat and bought a four-bedroom detached house for £500,000. They made a £100,00 deposit which they received from selling the flat. Rest of the money was paid by taking a mortgage. As Sarah decided that she would not go back to work but start her own accountancy farm, both she and Brian agreed that the house and mortgage would be in Brian's sole name to protect the house from any debt if Sarah's accountancy business was to suffer any loss. In return, Brian promised that the house would be Sarah's home – as much his as it was hers. Brian took the responsibility for mortgage repayments and Sarah took the responsibility to pay the household bills and childcare expenses.

In 2019, Sarah started her accountancy business. While the business was slowly growing due to the COVID-19 pandemic it suffered losses and as a result she decided to close down the accountancy business in 2020. She also found out that Brian was having an affair with his business partner. For this reason, Sarah decided that she no longer wishes to live with Brian. Similarly, Brian wanted to live with her lover. So, they both decided to sell the house.

Advise Brian and Sarah as to the beneficial entitlement to the house. Would their entitlement differ if both of them were registered proprietors of the house?

Answer: See the companion website.

Chapter 5: Co-ownership 2: Trust of land

Abraham (30), Bianca (28), Charlotte (25), David (22), and Emily (17) are siblings. A five-bedroom house was left to them by their grandparents in a will. The will stated that the house was conveyed to all five of them jointly.

Abraham does not get on very well with his siblings. He also turned to uncontrolled gambling and drinking. As a result of this, he got into financial difficulties and eventually became bankrupt.

Bianca works for a local accountancy firm, so she loves living in the area. She is also in a relationship with her boyfriend and wants to buy a house to live with him. However, Bianca understood that she would need a hefty deposit to pay in order to buy a house of their own. So, she thought that if she sold her share in the house that her grandparents left, she could get the deposit. So, she wrote a letter to Charlotte and David asking them if they were interested to buy her out. She included in the letter that a local estate agent valued the house at £500,000. She left the letter on the dining table addressed to Charlotte and David.

Before Charlotte and David had a chance to read the letter Emily found it. She was very angry and furious by knowing that her sister had offered her share of the house to Charlotte and David but not to her. She found Bianca upstairs just outside of her bedroom and confronted her. They both were arguing and at one point Emily pushed Bianca down the stairs and killed her. Emily has been charged for murdering Bianca and currently awaiting trial by jury in the Crown Court.

David was very upset by this incident and particularly the death of Bianca. He decided to sell his share in the house and approached Charlotte to see if she was interested to buy him out. Charlotte said that she has just started a new job as a probationer, and she is not sure if she could afford to buy him out. However, Charlotte said to him that she would apply for a mortgage in principle with her bank and if she gets a mortgage offer she would negotiate the price with him. Last month, Charlotte died in a car accident. After her death, a will was found in her bedroom cupboard drawer where she left all her property to her girlfriend, Chloe.

David is now unsure what will happen to the property now. He wants to know what shares he and others have in the house. He also wants to know if the house will have to be sold.

Answer: See the companion website.

Chapter 6: The law of leases

In January 2022, Jemina saw a notice in her local off-licence window advertising a 'room in a shared house'. She contacted and arranged to meet the owner, Avery. Avery told Jemina that she does not live in the property but rents it out. Jemina viewed a double room in the three-bedroom house. Jemina liked the room, but she wanted to know who else was living there. Avery told her that another person, Umar, lives in the other double bedroom, and the single bedroom is vacant. She also told her that, she does not want to rent the single bedroom because she keeps unused furniture in that room. Jemina asked if Avery would need to ask Umar's permission before she can move in. Avery said, 'no permission is needed as I am the landlord I decide who lives here and who does not'.

Avery asked for a £300 rent per week due on Friday each week to which Jemina agreed. She told Jemina that this is the rent for the whole flat and she is happy for Jemina and Umar to share this rent between them. However, if one of them fails to pay she should be able to claim the whole rent from either of them. She then showed Jemina the kitchen and communal areas. Jemina moved in.

Jemina and Umar were not getting on very well with each other as housemates. They had disagreements about cleaning and using the kitchen and the communal area. After six months Umar moved out. Jemina wanted her best friend Niamh to move with her and to take Umar's place. She called Avery for permission who was happy for Niamh to move in. Once Niamh moved in, Avery sent separate agreements to Jemina and Niamh. The terms of the agreements were the same and headed 'Occupancy Agreement'. The terms were as follows:

1. The parties agree that this is an occupancy agreement not a tenancy.
2. Avery is a licensor and Jemina/Umar is a licensee.
3. Avery can at all reasonable times enter the premises to inspect the property.
4. The licence fee in respect of the house is £300 per week.
5. If either licensee should move out and the other remains, the other is to be responsible for payment of the entire licence fee until a replacement occupier is found.
6. The licensor will clean the flat on each weekday at a mutually convenient time.
7. This agreement is to continue no longer than the duration of the COVID-19 pandemic but is subject to early termination by two weeks' notice if a cure is available for the members of the public against COVID.

Avery, Jemina, and Niamh signed the agreement. In June 2022, Avery sent a letter to both Jemina and Niamh where she stated that from 1 July 2022 you must pay £350 fee per week, if you fail to pay you have 2 weeks' time to vacate the house. If either of you keep living in the house, I would assume that the person living has agreed to pay the increased fee by herself. She also stated that because there are now vaccines available for protection against COVID-19, she can terminate the licence agreement under clause (vii) of the occupancy agreement.

Advise Jemina and Niamh if they occupy the flat under a lease or a licence.

Answer: See the companion website.

Chapter 7: Licences and proprietary estoppel

In February 2019, Jemina received a phone call from her father, Mohammad. Mohammad spoke to her every week about how he was getting on with life. On this occasion, he told Jemina that he is not very well and hardly able to move due to the longstanding ligament damage in his legs. Jemina replied that she wished she could help but she has just started a new job in London so could not help. Mohammad told her that if she comes to live with Mohammad and take care of him he will ensure that she is well provided for when he is gone.

In June 2019, Jemina resigned from her job as a trainee accountant and moved into Mohammad's house. Since then, Jemina had been taking care of Mohammad, doing the shopping, and looking after the house as well. Jemina believed that she should not only take care of Mohammad but also the house as it will be hers after Mohammad's death. In April 2021 Mohammad died. His will left the house to his son Umar and £10,000 to Jemina.

Advise Jemina as to whether she has any interest in the house.

Answer: See the companion website.

Chapter 8: Easements and *profits á prendre*

Jemina inherited a plot of two acres from her parents. There was a house in the plot situated at the far end. The house had a small garden in front. The house was accessible from a private road that ran across the plot and joined the main road. In 2010, Jemina sold the house with the small garden to Umar. Jemina kept the rest of the plot. Umar was using the same road to access the house from the main road as Jemina did. The deed of sale to Umar included a clause where Jemina retained a right to use the private road.

In 2015, Jemina built a house on the retained part of the land. The house had a common fence between Jemina and Umar. Both Umar and Jemina maintained the fence. However, to maintain the back of the house Umar needed to go onto Jemina's retained land.

In 2019, Umar lost his job so he wanted to let the 'guest area' of his house. In the lease agreement, Umar agreed to let the 'guest area' to Avery with a permission to park her car in the car park located in front of the small garden of the house. In 2020, Umar granted Avery a six-month lease of the guest area which was later renewed for another three years.

In 2022, the relationship between Jemina, Umar, and Avery deteriorated. Jemina asked Umar to pay £1,000 per year to use the private road. In response, Umar stopped maintaining the fence between the houses. In retaliation, Jemina wrote to Umar that he can no longer use her land to maintain the back of his house. The lack of maintenance has caused the house damage, which includes window and door frames that have started to rot, and heavy rain damaged the gutter. Umar also told Avery to stop parking her car in the car park.

Can any of these rights be enforced?

Answer: See the companion website.

Chapter 9: Freehold covenants

Jemina is the registered owner of a manor house which also has a converted barn located in the southern corner of the property. To renovate the old manor house, she sold the converted barn to Umar in 2018. In the deed of transfer, Jemina granted Umar a right of way over the main driveway which connected the barn's car park with the main road outside of the manor's main gate. The driveway also connected the manor's car park with the main road. The deed also included the following restrictions:

- Umar to pay one half of the cost of maintaining the driveway.
- Umar to use the property only for the purpose of a single private dwelling.
- Umar to keep the boundary fence in good repair.
- Umar to lend Jemina a book every week from his personal library collection.

Umar sold the barn to Emily in 2020 who started to run a B&B business. In 2021, Jemina sold the manor house to Jack who is very annoyed with Emily's B&B business. He thinks the B&B guests made a lot of noise. He is also annoyed by being repeatedly refused by Emily to contribute to the maintenance cost of the driveway and repair the fence. She also refused to lend any more books to Jack.

Advise Jack.

Answer: See the companion website.

Chapter 10: Adverse possession

Jemina purchased 1 Wimbledon Terrace, a registered land, in December 2007. Her next-door neighbour is Avery who is the owner of 2 Wimbledon Terrace, a registered land. Avery's neighbour is Niamh who is the owner of 3 Wimbledon Terrace, an unregistered land.

Jemina loves gardening and her garden at 1 Wimbledon Terrace is full of flower beds and vegetable patches. She wanted more space to expand her garden and she saw that her next-door neighbour Avery has not used most of her garden space. She thought that it would be good to have some of those unused spaces in Avery's Garden. In June 2008, Jemina trimmed the overgrown shrubs in Avery's Garden. In December 2008, she put her Barbeque grill in the garden. In February 2009, Jemina put up a fence around some of the unused strips of Avery's Garden. There was no challenge or objection from Avery.

There was no fence between Avery's and Niamh's Garden. In June 2009, Avery put up a fence between her and Niamh's Garden. The builder that erected the fence was not sure about the boundary but mistakenly thought that the boundary should be erected on the other side of the hedges that are currently dividing the gardens. As a result, a small strip of land from Niamh's Garden was taken by the erected fence.

Advise Jemina, Avery, and Niamh about their legal position with respect to the boundaries of their gardens.

Answer: See the companion website.

Chapter 11: Mortgages

You are instructed by a married couple who have three young children. The couple want to buy a four-bedroom house by selling the flat where they are currently living. They have received an offer from a potential buyer who wants to buy the flat. The couple have also found a four-bedroom house which they would like to buy. You have been asked to act as a solicitor to exchange contract and complete the purchase of the house. You have been told that the deposit money would come from the sale of the flat and the rest of the money from mortgage. You have been asked by the couple to find or recommend a lender. You have conducted a search and found Moneyhive as a potential lender which you recommended to the couple.

A few days later the business manager of Moneyhive contacted you to represent them in a number of mortgage deals which included the one which you suggested for the couple. You thought that you should discuss this with the couple before getting back to the business manager of Moneyhive. So, you booked an appointment for the next day. While having a conversation with the husband you found out that he was having a clandestine affair with another woman. What are you going to do? Please ensure that your responses are in accordance with the SRA's professional code of conduct.

Answer: See the companion website.

Appendix C

Multiple choice questions (MCQs) and answers

Chapter 1: Preliminary Information before you start studying Land law for SQE1

Sanjay is the registered proprietor of an old manor house with an oval-shaped garden around it. He wanted to attract potential caravaners to park their caravans in the garden of the house. He also wanted to rent out a few rooms of the house to holidaymakers. So, he decided to carry out some renovation works in the house and garden. The renovation works carried out included laying out new carpets, fitting a new central heating system, and installing pre-paid electric charging ports for the caravaners. Although the business was doing very well during the summer it suffered loss during the winter and did not attract many holidaymakers and caravaners to the house and its adjoining garden. Hence, he decided to sell the house and garden. Peppa bought the house and garden but when she moved in she found that Sanjay has removed the carpets, the radiators, and combi boiler from the central heating system, and the electric sockets from the property.

Which one of the following best explains the likely outcome for Peppa?

A. Sanjay needs to refit the carpets, reinstall the radiators, combi boiler, and electric sockets because these are fixtures and accordingly constitute parts of the land that is sold to Peppa.

B. Sanjay does not need to refit the carpets and reinstall the radiators, combi boiler, and electric sockets because these are chattels and accordingly do not constitute parts of the land that is sold to Peppa.

C. Sanjay does not need to refit the carpets or reinstall the electric sockets because these are chattels and accordingly do not constitute parts of the land that is sold to Peppa. However, he needs to reinstall the radiators and combi boiler as these are fixtures and accordingly constitute parts of the land.

D. Sanjay does not need to refit the carpets or reinstall the radiators and combi boiler because these are chattels and accordingly do not constitute parts of the land that is sold to Peppa. However, he needs to reinstall the electric sockets as these are fixtures and accordingly constitute a part of the land.

DOI: 10.4324/9781003204954-14

E. Sanjay does not need to reinstall the radiators, combi boiler, and electric sockets because these are chattels and accordingly do not constitute parts of the land that is sold to Peppa. However, he needs to refit the carpets as these are fixtures and accordingly constitute a part of the land.

Answer:

A is incorrect. The carpets, radiators, combi boiler, and electric sockets are not all fixtures.

B is incorrect. The carpets, radiators, combi boiler, and electric sockets are not all chattels.

C is CORRECT. Sanjay sold a land which included fixtures but not chattels. By applying the common law principles in relation to fixtures and chattels (degree and purpose of annexation) it can be concluded that the carpets and electric sockets are chattels, but the radiators and combi boiler are fixtures. This is because the radiators and combi boiler are being attached to a wall of the house, they are a permanent part of the land. However, the carpets and electric sockets were not permanent parts of the land because they were not fitted for permanent use or benefit of the land but for beneficial enjoyment of the previous owner and his business. Therefore, Sanjay would only need to reinstall the radiators and combi boiler but would not need to refit the carpets or reinstall the electric sockets.

D is incorrect. The radiators and combi boiler are fixtures, so these must be reinstalled. Also, the electric sockets are chattels so do not need to be reinstalled.

E is incorrect. See above.

Chapter 2: Unregistered Land law

1. Alan owns Green Gables (a large house with extensive grounds). He builds a cottage on part of the grounds and sells it to Bill in fee simple. In the conveyance to Bill in 2020 he imposes a restrictive covenant to prevent Bill from carrying on a business on the land. If Bill sells the cottage (unregistered land) to Cath, will she be bound by the covenant? Please choose TWO correct answers from the following options:

   (a) Cath will be bound by the covenant under the doctrine of notice even if the covenant has not been registered as a land charge.
   (b) Cath will be bound by the covenant if it is registered as a D (ii) land charge, and she has purchased a legal estate in the cottage.
   (c) Cath will be bound by the covenant even if she has purchased an equitable estate in the cottage.
   (d) Cath will not be bound by the covenant if she was unaware of the covenant.
   (e) Cath will not be bound by the covenant if it is registered in the wrong name, and she has searched against the correct name of the owners who owned the property for last 15 years.

Answer: (a) is INCORRECT – as doctrine of notice does not apply here.

(b) is CORRECT – according to Sections 2 and 4(6) of LCA 1972 which require registration of the land charge, and a purchase of a legal estate.

(c) is INCORRECT – as above – purchasing an equitable interest would not suffice.

(d) is INCORRECT – awareness does not have any consequences as provided by S. 4(6) of the LCA 1972.

(e) is CORRECT – as Cathy has searched against the correct name of the owners who owned the cottage for the last 15 years (the root of title); see also *Diligent Finance Company v Alleyne* in (1971) 23 P & CR 346.

2. In the above scenario, assume that Alan holds Green Gables on trust for his adult daughters, Ethel and Freda. If David buys Green Gables from Alan, will he be bound by the daughters' interests in the property? Select the CORRECT answer:
   (a) David will be bound because the doctrine of notice will automatically apply.
   (b) David will be bound as he has not overreached the beneficial interest of his daughters by making payment of the purchase price to at least two trustees.
   (c) David will be bound if he is aware of the beneficial interest under the doctrine of notice as he has not overreached the beneficial interest of his daughters by making payment of the purchase price to at least two trustees.
   (d) David will not be bound as the daughters' beneficial interests were not registered as land charges.
   (e) David will not be bound as he was not aware of the daughters' beneficial interest in the cottage.

Answer: (a) is INCORRECT – as doctrine of notice does not automatically apply here. It only applies if the overreaching failed.

(b) is INCORRECT – David is not bound by the daughters' beneficial interest merely because overreaching did not occur but the application of the doctrine of notice is necessary.

(c) is CORRECT – as above – both the failure of overreaching and the application of the doctrine of notice will apply.

(d) is INCORRECT – the daughters' beneficial interests are not registrable under the LCA 1972.

(e) is INCORRECT – mere unawareness would not suffice because the doctrine of notice imposes a constructive notice, see *Kingsnorth Finance Co. Ltd v Tizard* [1986] 1 WLR 783.

Chapter 3: Registration of title

1. Wendy lives in Wren Cottage, the matrimonial home, of which her husband, Habib, was the registered proprietor with absolute title. In 2021, Habib deserted

Wendy and mortgaged the cottage to a bank. The mortgage payments were well in arrears and the bank seeks possession of the cottage. Wendy, who gave Habib £10,000 towards the purchase-price of the cottage, refuses to leave. Which of the following options **are** CORRECT:

(a) Wendy cannot refuse to leave because she is not a registered proprietor of Wren cottage.
(b) Wendy cannot refuse to leave because the bank has a legal interest in the cottage.
(c) Wendy can refuse to leave the cottage if she has an overriding interest by actual occupation and she has entered that interest as a notice in the land register.
(d) Wendy can refuse to leave if she can establish an overriding interest by actual occupation and she does not need to enter this into the land register as a notice.
(e) Wendy can refuse to leave because the bank is a mortgagee but not a purchaser, so they do not have priority over her interest in the cottage.

Answer: (a) is INCORRECT – because the protection of Wendy's interest is not dependent on her status as a registered proprietor.
(b) is INCORRECT – according to Section 29 of LRA 2002 the bank is subject to any overriding interest such as Wendy's.
(c) is CORRECT – Wendy is not required by law to enter her overriding interest by entry of a notice but she can do that if she wants to warn a new purchaser. That means the law encourages her to do that, but she is not bound.
(d) is CORRECT – as above her overriding interest by actual occupation is protected without registration.
(e) is INCORRECT – the bank is not only a mortgagee but also a purchaser so they have priority under the basic rule.

2. Which of the following statements are correct:
   (a) A purchaser of land by fraud is bound by any equitable interests occurring prior to that purchase, as the transaction was not made by valuable consideration.
   (b) A purchaser of land by fraud is not bound by any equitable interests occurred prior to that purchase, as the transaction was not made by valuable consideration.
   (c) A purchaser has priority over all interests except those entered on the register and those overriding within Schedule 3.
   (d) A court or registrar can decide the priority of a purchaser against the basic and special priority rules, if doing that would give the party the priority which it should have had but for the mistake.
   (e) A victim of fraud cannot claim any indemnity from the Land Registry because s/he is not protected from fraudulent entry in the register.

Answer: (a) is CORRECT – because the law does not treat a fraudulent transaction as made with a valuable consideration. See *Halifax v Popeck [2008] All ER 281*.
(b) is INCORRECT – as above.
(c) is CORRECT – see the basic rule of priority under Section 28 of the LRA 2002.
(d) is CORRECT – see the clarification of Schedule 4 paragraph 8 in *Gold Harp v Macleod [2014] EWCA Civ 532*.
(e) is INCORRECT – according to the insurance principle, a victim of fraud can claim indemnity from the Land Registry.

Chapter 4: Co-ownership 1: Informal acquisition of Title (Implied trusts)

Sarah lives in Green Cottage, a matrimonial home, of which both she and her husband, Brian, are the registered proprietors. They each paid half of the deposit. Brian paid the monthly mortgage payments and Sarah paid the household bills. The relationship broke down in 2021. They both wanted to sell the cottage. Which one of the following is INCORRECT?

(a) The law presumes that both Brian and Sarah are joint tenants in law and equity.
(b) The presumption that both Brian and Sarah are joint tenants in law and equity is rebuttable.
(c) In the absence of a common intention, the court can infer a fair share between the co-owners.
(d) In the absence of a common intention and where an inference is impossible or unconscionable, the court can impute a fair share between the co-owners.
(e) The court can allocate shares according to the contribution of co-owners in the purchase price.

Answer: (a) is CORRECT – the law presumes this in joint name cases.
(b) is CORRECT – this is a rebuttable presumption: see *Stack v Dowden*.
(c) is CORRECT – the court can infer a fair share in the absence of a common intention: see *Jones v Kernott*.
(d) is CORRECT – the court can impute by taking into account the whole course of conduct between the parties: see *Aspden v Elvy*.
(e) is INCORRECT – this is incorrect as the law in *Lloyds Bank v Rossett* has now changed. The allocation of share now depends on the conduct of the parties which include changing of a common intention in course of time and financial arrangements of the co-owners.

Chapter 5: Co-ownership 2: Trust of land

1. Abu dies leaving his property in a will in joint names of Bevan (24) and Christy (22). The will does not state what shares they are given. Which of the following is CORRECT?

(a) The property is held by Bevan and Christy as joint tenants.
(b) The property is held by Bevan and Christy as tenants in common.
(c) The ownership of the property cannot pass to Bevan and Christy because it was given to them by a will.
(d) Bevan is a legal owner and Christy is an equitable owner.
(e) Bevan is an equitable owner and Christy is a legal owner.

Answer: (a) is CORRECT – the law presumes that the property is left to Bevan and Christy as joint tenants.
(b) is INCORRECT – as their shares have not been allocated in the will, the property is held under a joint tenancy not tenancy in common.
(c) is INCORRECT – co-ownership of a property can be created by a will.
(d) is INCORRECT – as the will stated both of their name both of them are legal owner unless one of them has not attained full age. The facts stated that they are both attained the age of majority.
(e) is INCORRECT – see above.

2. In the above scenario, Christy gives notice to Bevan in writing to state that she wants to sell her share in the property. She insists that she is entitled to half of the share of the property as it was left to the two of them, so it makes sense that Abu gave each of them a half share. Which of the following are INCORRECT?
   (a) Christy is not entitled to half of the property in the absence of an express allocation in the will.
   (b) Christy and Bevan are joint tenants so they will have to convert the property by severance before selling.
   (c) Christy has not severed her share by giving written notice to Bevan that she wants to sell her share unless Bevan has accepted this.
   (d) Christy does not have to give a notice in writing to Bevan as she can just sell her share.
   (e) Bevan cannot go to court to stop the sale of the property if Christy so wishes.

Answer: (a) is CORRECT – the law presumes that the property is left to Bevan and Christy as joint tenants so Christy is not entitled to half of the share of the property in the absence of a clear intention of Abu. In this case, the court shall decide a fair share between them.
(b) is CORRECT – as they are joint tenants they will have to sever the property before selling.
(c) is CORRECT – severance is possible by giving written notice to other joint tenants. As Bevan is the only other joint tenant here, the notice in writing has severed the joint tenancy to a tenancy in common. However, a court order would be necessary in the absence of a clear intention from Abu, and if Bevan disagrees with Christy about their respective shares in the property. The answer is correct because if Bevan refuses to buy Christy out, no severance would occur.

(d) is INCORRECT – notice in writing is a key requirement to sever Christy's share.
(e) is INCORRECT – Bevan can go to the court for an order to stop the sale by Christy under Sections 14 and 15 of the TOLATA.

Chapter 6: Landlord and tenant (The law of leases)

Jemina granted Umar a lease (in a deed) of her studio flat for five years at a market rent. The agreement is titled 'licence agreement'. Which one of the following is CORRECT?

(a) The lease is an equitable lease because it has not been registered.
(b) The agreement is not a lease because it does not state if exclusive possession has been granted.
(c) The agreement is not a lease because the rent has not been specifically set out.
(d) The agreement is a licence because its title is 'licence agreement'.
(e) The agreement is a lease because the term is certain for five years, exclusive possession can be implied, and market rent has been specified – all meet the legal requirement.

Answer: (a) is INCORRECT – because a lease for seven years or under does not need registration to be legal, the only requirement for a lease over three years is that it has to be made in a deed: see LP (MP) 1989, S. 1; LPA 1925, Ss. 52(1) (2) (d), 54 (d).
(b) is INCORRECT – exclusive possession can be inferred from the circumstances so it is not necessary for the parties to specifically include in the agreement: see *Berrisford v Mexfield* (2011) UKSC 52.
(c) is INCORRECT – it is not necessary for the rent to set out specifically. As long as a rent is set to a certain standard, i.e., market rent, that would suffice. See *Street v Mountford* (1985) AC 809.
(d) is INCORRECT – labelling an agreement is not conclusive but the circumstances under which the agreement was concluded: see *Antoniades v Villiers* (1990) 1 AC 417.
(e) is CORRECT – this is correct because it meets the three key characteristics of a lease such as exclusive possession, a term certain, and a rent.

Chapter 7: Licences and proprietary estoppel

In which of the following situations an interest under proprietary estoppel will arise?

(a) A claimant will be able to establish an estoppel if they can prove an assurance, reliance, and detriment in circumstances in which it would be unconscionable to deny a remedy to the claimant.
(b) A claimant will be able to establish an estoppel only if the assurance or promise has been expressly communicated to them.

(c) A claimant will be able to establish an estoppel if the detriment occurred, irrespective of whether such occurrence was the result of the reliance or not.
(d) A claimant will be able to establish an estoppel where the promise is not directly made to him.
(e) A claimant will be able to establish an estoppel to enforce an oral agreement which the parties intended but failed to conclude in writing.

Answer: (a) is CORRECT – because assurance, reliance, detriment, and unconscionability are the four criteria to successfully claim a PE: see *Taylor Fashions v Liverpool Victoria Trustees* (1982) QB 133.
(b) is INCORRECT – because the promise or assurance can be express and/or implied. It is not necessary for the promise to be expressly communicated.
(c) is INCORRECT – because the detrimental reliance must have been caused due to the promise. An independent determinant that has not resulted from the reliance would not suffice: see *Orgee v Orgee* [1997] EGCS 152.
(d) is INCORRECT – because promises must be made to the claimant in order to make a successful claim for PE: see *Lloyd v Dugdale* [2001] EWCA Civ 1754.
(e) is INCORRECT – a claimant cannot enforce an oral agreement in a PE claim but it is possible to do that in a Constructive Trust claim: see *Matchmove v Dowding* [2016] EWCA Civ 1233.

Chapter 8: Easements and *profits à prendre*

In 2012, Jemina, the registered freehold owner of a farm, granted certain rights *by deed*. Please identify which of the following grants are easements:

(a) Avery (a neighbour), the right to park her car in the car park of the farm.
(b) Bianca (another neighbour), the right to use the swimming pool on the farm in the afternoon of each and every weekend as she does not have a swimming pool on her land.
(c) Umar, the right to collect half a tonne of pineapples each and every year from the farm.
(d) Niamh (a neighbouring farmer who occupies land a few miles away), the right to store up to 15 tonnes of coal in the storage of the farm.
(e) Mohammad (not a neighbour), the right to store a tonne of hay in the main shed of the farm.

Answer: (a) is an easement – because a right to park can be capable of being an easement by an express grant.
(b) is an easement – because this can be capable of being an easement and is beneficial for the enjoyment of Bianca's land. It can be argued as a recreational easement.
(c) is NOT an easement – this is more like a personal right which is not capable of being an easement: see *Re Ellenborough Park* (1956) Ch 131. However, this can be argued as a profit.

(d) May NOT be an easement – because it is possible to have a right to store goods on one's neighbour's land provided one does not try to store too much. As 15 tonnes can be a quantity too much that may impose a burden it can be argued that this right cannot be an easement.
(e) is NOT an easement – because this is more personal right from which Mohammad may benefit but not his land: see *Hill v Tupper* (1863) 2 H & C 121. Also, he is not a neighbour.

Chapter 9: Freehold covenants

Acorn Builders Ltd owned a freehold land on London Road. They divided the land into three plots and sold them to three different buyers. Each transfer of the plots was by deed. The deed included a covenant which provided that 'the property must be used as a single private family home'. Umar recently purchased one of the plots and started to run his accountancy business from the property. Which of the following are CORRECT:

(a) Umar is not bound to comply with the covenant because he was not one of the parties who originally accepted it.
(b) Umar is not bound to comply with the covenant because it is a positive covenant which passed on to the successor in title.
(c) Umar is bound to comply with the covenant because the burden of a restrictive covenant passed on to him in equity.
(d) Umar is bound to comply with the covenant, but he can make an application to the Upper Tribunal to discharge or modify the covenant as this is deemed to be obsolete.
(e) Umar can escape from his burden to comply with the covenant under the Contract (Rights of Third Parties) Act 1999.

Answer: (a) is INCORRECT – because the burden to a restrictive covenant passes to the successors in title in equity.
(b) is INCORRECT – because it is a negative covenant although the words used sound positive.
(c) is CORRECT – see explanation in (a).
(d) is CORRECT – because an application can be made to discharge or modify a restrictive covenant under Section 84 of the Law of Property Act 1925.
(e) is INCORRECT – because the 1999 Act enables a third party such as other plot owners to enforce the covenants as long as there was no intention by the original parties to the contrary. As this is a building scheme, such an intention can be apparent: see Section 56 LPA 1925.

Chapter 10: Adverse possession

Which of the following positions, in relation to adverse possession, are legally CORRECT:

(a) An adverse possessor will have to complete 12 years of adverse possession in order to become a paper owner if the disputed land is registered.
(b) An adverse possessor will have to complete 12 years of adverse possession in order to become a paper owner if the disputed land is unregistered.
(c) An adverse possessor will have to complete ten years of adverse possession in order to make an application to become the registered proprietor if the disputed land is registered.
(d) An adverse possessor will have to complete ten years of adverse possession in order to make an application to become the registered proprietor if the disputed land is unregistered.
(e) Irrespective of the nature of the disputed land, i.e., registered or unregistered, an adverse possession claim must establish that they have completed 12 years of adverse possession.

Answer: (a) is INCORRECT – because the required period of adverse possession for registered land is 10 years. Also, completion of this period does not guarantee title.
(b) is CORRECT – because the required period of adverse possession for unregistered land is 12 years. See the Limitation Act 1980.
(c) is CORRECT – see explanation in (a).
(d) is INCORRECT – see explanation in (b).
(e) is INCORRECT – because the applicable laws for adverse possession in registered and unregistered land are different. See the explanation in (a) and (b).

Chapter 11: Mortgages

Which of the following are CORRECT when a mortgagor of a residential property defaulted to make repayments:

(a) The mortgagee can sell the property straightaway to recover the outstanding debt.
(b) The mortgagee will have to send a written notice of default to the mortgagor and cannot sell the mortgaged property until three months passed since the notice was issued and no payments were made.
(c) The mortgagee would need to bring a possession proceeding before selling the mortgaged property.
(d) In a possession proceeding the court cannot take into account the social and economic interests of the mortgagor in determining the question of possession.
(e) In a possession proceeding the court can take into account the social and economic interests of the mortgagor under the Consumer Credit Act 1974.

Answer: (a) is INCORRECT – Because a mortgagee cannot sell the mortgaged property straightaway but will have to give notice of default to the mortgagor, wait for another three months, and the mortgage failed to make any payments in those three months: See LPA, S. 103.

(b) is CORRECT – see explanation in (a).
(c) is CORRECT – because a sale of the property is only viable once a vacant possession is obtained in respect to the property. It is problematic and may not attract potential buyers if the mortgaged property is occupied by a defaulted mortgagor.
(d) is INCORRECT – because under the Consumer Credit Act the court has a wider discretion and can take into account social and economic interests of the mortgagor.
(e) is CORRECT – see explanation in (d).

Index

For Product Safety Concerns and Information please contact our EU representative GPSR@taylorandfrancis.com Taylor & Francis Verlag GmbH, Kaufingerstraße 24, 80331 München, Germany